Spiritual Leadership in Action

The CEL Story

Achieving Extraordinary Results
Through Ordinary People

A volume in
Advances in Workplace Spirituality: Theory, Research, and Practice
Louis W. Fry, *Series Editor*

Spiritual Leadership in Action

The CEL Story
Achieving Extraordinary Results
Through Ordinary People

Louis W. Fry

Texas A&M University–Central Texas

Yochanan Altman

Bordeaux Management School

INFORMATION AGE PUBLISHING, INC.
Charlotte, NC • www.infoagepub.com

Library of Congress Cataloging-in-Publication Data

A CIP record for this book is available from the Library of Congress
http://www.loc.gov

ISBN: 978-1-62396-409-2 (Paperback)
         978-1-62396-410-8 (Hardcover)
         978-1-62396-411-5 (ebook)

*With the consent of the authors, Lynne Sedgmore
has this book dedicated to CEL staff in thanks and gratitude.
Without every single one of you, this book could not have been written.
An individual leader's journey is only as powerful and effective as the individuals
and community she leads and is a member of. We are all simultaneously the
synergy and the parts, as well as our own unique contribution to the whole.*

Contents

Series Introduction

A major change is taking place in the personal and professional lives of many organizational leaders and their employees as they aspire to integrate their spirituality and religion with their work. Many argue that the reason behind this change is that society is seeking spiritual solutions to better respond to tumultuous social, business, geopolitical changes. The result has been a remarkable explosion of scholarship that provides the opportunity for more specialized interest areas, including the role of spirituality and religion in shaping organizations: structures, decision making, management style, mission and strategy, organizational culture, human resource management, finance and accounting, marketing and sales—in short: all aspects of leading, managing, and organizing resources and people. As evidenced in the mainstream acceptance of the *Journal of Management, Spirituality and Religion* and the success of the Management, Spirituality, and Religion Special Interest Group of the *Academy of Management,* an emerging field with a broad focus on workplace spirituality is gathering momentum.

This book series, *Advances in Workplace Spirituality: Theory, Research, and Application,* focuses on the study of the relationship and relevance of spirituality and/or religion to organizational life. Its vision is to draw from a diverse range of scholarly areas to become a pivotal source for integrative theory, research and application on workplace spirituality. The purpose of the series is to (1) provide scholars with a meaningful collection of books in key areas and create a forum for the field, (2) support a growing trend toward paradigm integration and assimilation through the interdisciplinary

Spiritual Leadership in Action, pages xi–xii
Copyright © 2013 by Information Age Publishing
All rights of reproduction in any form reserved.

nature of this series, and (3) draw from a wide variety of disciplines for integrative thinking on workplace spirituality with the broad goal of adding to the value of workplace spirituality theory, research, and its application. The series aims to serve as a meeting forum and help cross-fertilization in these communities. Our sole criterion is academic rigor and scientific merit.

The third book of this series is a case study that illustrates the marriage between the theory, research, and practice of workplace spirituality. In doing so, *Spiritual Leadership in Action: The CEL Story*, draws from the emerging fields of workplace spirituality, spiritual leadership, sustainability, and performance excellence. This book is designed for thoughtful leaders working in the complexity and messiness of their daily organizational lives. It is the story of a CEO leader and the integration of her spiritual yearning and fulfillment manifested through her professional vocation and calling—a case study containing features, dilemmas and opportunities facing all leaders today. It is also a practical book with reflections, legacy and "lessons learnt" to support and guide busy leaders who are looking for wisdom and to learn from the experiences and mistakes of others. First and foremost though this is a story about people, about the ways they find purpose, creativity and meaning in their professional work; how they thrive in community and fulfill their deep desire to be of service to others against seemingly impossible odds and limitations. It illustrates how, by implementing spirituality in the workplace through spiritual leadership, full human potential and creativity is released and how the spirit within, and without, can be experienced and manifested.

—**Louis W. (Jody) Fry**

Series Editor

Foreword

In 1997 I published the report *Learning Works*. It was the product of three years work for the Further Education Council looking at widening participation, and it opened my eyes to another world. During that period I immersed myself in sixth form and further education (FE) colleges as well as adult education institutions. The upshot was that I fell in love with the sector. I have always been a passionate advocate and supporter of FE because I knew what it meant to the life chances of members of my family. But it was seeing at close hand the transformative work that is done with both young and adult learners from multiple backgrounds, with a wide range of talents and possibilities, that was so awe inspiring. It confirmed for me that the FE role in social mobility, economic prosperity, and raised aspirations is critical to the wellbeing of our communities.

None of it is possible without wonderful people. We are all aware of the importance of teaching and support staff in ensuring the success of learners and the pivotal place of good leaders in creating an environment of empowerment and innovation, but the challenge is "how do we get there?" This story of the leadership and courage in the Centre for Excellence in Leadership is both instructive and heart-warming. I am struck by the collective nature of the journey with a dedicated and talented group of staff doing their absolute best to serve their customers, stakeholders, and learners, experimenting along the way, and fostering a new level of spirit and excellence to achieve impressive outcomes.

Spiritual Leadership in Action, pages xiii–xiv
Copyright © 2013 by Information Age Publishing
All rights of reproduction in any form reserved.

Lynne Sedgmore's professional and personal story is itself uplifting and hugely impressive. She has been a powerful leader in FE for over 30 years. Yet she herself acknowledges that she is but one of many seminal voices in the book—the CEL board members, the senior leadership team, indeed every one of the staff, full- and part-time, played their role in this success. Many, but not all, are named, but I honor them all. This was a collective endeavor.

It is invaluable that the process was researched by such eminent academics in the field of spiritual leadership, and that is a clear testament to the uniqueness and value of the work of CEL. For such a detailed and fascinating case study to be published leaves a precious legacy—a really important contribution to our understanding of what makes for good leadership. There is much to learn in this compelling book, and I hope you enjoy reading it.

I am also delighted that the royalties of the book will be given to the charity that bears my name—the Helena Kennedy Foundation—which exists to overcome social injustice by providing financial bursaries, mentoring, and support to disadvantaged students from the further and adult education sectors. It enables people to complete their studies in higher education and move on successfully into employment. The charity's founder, my good friend Ann Limb, was a trustee of CEL and played a significant part in its journey of spirit and success. The chain of connections is strong, and it means that this book will definitely make a contribution to changing lives.

—Baroness Helena Kennedy of the Shaws QC

Introduction

O ne of the greatest challenges facing leaders of both large and small organizations today is to develop business models that address the diverse business issues of ethical leadership, employee wellbeing, sustainability, and social responsibility without sacrificing profitability, revenue growth, and other metrics of performance excellence—the triple bottom line or "people, planet, and profit." In this regard, feature articles from *Newsweek, Time, Fortune,* and *Business Week* have chronicled the growing presence of spirituality in the corporate world and its relevance for this new business model. Patricia Abrudene (2007), in *Megatrends 2010: The Rise of Conscious Capitalism,* argues that a megatrend is taking place in the transformation of the personal and professional lives of many chief executive officers (CEOs) and leaders as they aspire to integrate their spirituality with their work. In many cases, this has led to very positive changes in their interpersonal relationships at work and to their organization's effectiveness.

Furthermore, there is evidence that workplace spirituality programs may be essential for the triple bottom line since they show promise not only for beneficial personal outcomes, such as increased positive human health and psychological wellbeing, but they deliver also improved employee commitment and productivity while reducing absenteeism and turnover. Plus, there is mounting evidence that a spiritual workplace is a foundation for performance excellence, flexibility, and innovation and is a source of sustainable competitive advantage. Thus there is a need today for books on organizations and their leaders who have developed business models that address this call for spirituality in the workplace.

Written for practitioners, *Spiritual Leadership in Action: The CEL Story* answers this call. This book is intended to illustrate the model of spiritual leadership recently introduced in the groundbreaking book *Maximizing the Triple Bottom Line Through Spiritual Leadership* (Fry & Nisiewicz, 2013), which summarizes over ten years of academic research in terms understandable to practitioners. In doing so, *Spiritual Leadership in Action: The CEL Story* draws from the emerging fields of workplace spirituality, spiritual leadership, sustainability, conscious capitalism, and performance excellence to present the first in-depth case study of such an organization—a ground-breaking case study based on rigorous qualitative and quantitative research.

This book is designed for thoughtful leaders working in the complexity and messiness of their daily organizational lives. It is a book first and foremost about people, about the ways they find purpose, creativity, and meaning in their professional work, how they thrive in community and fulfill their deep desires to be of service to others against seemingly impossible odds and limitations. This is a case study of how full human potential and creativity is released, how the spirit within, and without, can be experienced and manifested. It is a story of ordinary people achieving extraordinary results, individually and collectively; becoming more than they thought was possible; and having fun along the way.

It is also a practical book with reflections, legacy and "lessons learned" to support and guide busy leaders who are looking for wisdom and to learn from the experiences and mistakes of others. We live in turbulent, fast moving and extraordinary times where case studies and stories may be the best form of assistance as we weave our own leadership paths and footprints.

Spiritual Leadership in Action: The CEL Story is not a complex academic treatise, although it is the result of serious and rigorous academic research. Neither is it a magic recipe of numbered ingredients or secrets for surefire and quick success. It is a case study containing features, dilemmas and opportunities facing all leaders today. It is the leadership narrative of a professional community who learned to live and work together with respect and harmony. It is also the story of a CEO leader and the integration of her spiritual yearning and fulfillment manifested through her professional vocation and calling.

In particular, it explores how to:

- ▪ create effective collaborative partnerships;
- ▪ deliver outstanding value for money on limited resources in complex contexts;

- develop excellent commercial practices within a public sector organization; and
- nurture the spirit, high energy, and performance of everyone involved to ensure outstanding success on the triple bottom line.

This book encourages readers to be bold; creative; reflective; trusting; even more allowing of their own spirit and leadership paths, and to rise to even greater achievements; but most of all to fulfill their own deepest yearnings and potential and to become the very best of what they are meant to be, both as leaders and as human beings.

An important feature in this book is that spirituality and religion are distinct, and that organizational spiritual leadership can be inclusive or exclusive of religious theory and practice. The Centre for Excellence in Leadership (CEL) serves as a role model for maximizing the triple bottom line through both personal and organizational spiritual leadership. We believe CEL is a stellar example of an organization that embraced organizational spiritual leadership, the values of altruistic love, employee wellbeing, and sustainability while maintaining high levels of financial performance. Their CEO, Lynne Sedgmore, has a strong inner life and spiritual practice and has been open about her commitment to workplace spirituality and personal spiritual leadership. *Spiritual Leadership in Action: The CEL Story* chronicles how she led CEL through its spiritual journey, including several "dark nights of the soul," to a place of pre-eminence in the United Kingdom's learning and skills sector.

Spiritual Leadership in Action: The CEL Story examines organizational effectiveness and wellbeing in CEL through an in-depth study of the organization as seen by its principal stakeholders. A specific objective of this study was to examine the spiritual essence of CEL as a non-faith organization that strives to do good. We employed different research methods including interviews, focus groups, targeted participant observation, and two questionnaires: one for line managers concerning performance, the other covering a range of performance, wellbeing, and spirituality topics. Our study confirmed CEL as a high performing, high energy, and successful organization, displaying a passion for its mission and demonstrating consistency with the models of personal and organizational spiritual leadership and the spiritual leadership balanced scorecard business model.

We end with a discussion of CEL's legacy to point out how leaders and their organizations may draw on CEL's example. *Spiritual Leadership in Action: The CEL Story,* with its focus on fostering conscious, sustainable organizations that maximize the triple bottom line, offers a refreshing new example of how ordinary people, their organizations, and their leaders can redefine and achieve success in today's global, Internet age.

Roadmap for this Book

Each chapter concludes with a summary of key learning and practical tools to support our readers in fostering their own spiritual development, leadership capability, and organizational practice.

> Chapter 1—*The Beginning: Three Tribes Come Together to Turn Problems into Opportunity* provides an initial introduction to and general overview of the Centre for Excellence in Leadership and its CEO, Lynne Sedgmore. It then introduces a model of organizational spirituality that provides the context for subsequent discussion of the personal and organizational spiritual leadership models and the spiritual leadership balanced scorecard business model.

> Chapter 2—*The Journey of Personal Spiritual Leadership: CEL's CEO, Lynne Sedgmore* introduces and explains the personal spiritual leadership model and uses it as a framework to chronicle the beginning of Lynne Sedgmore's spiritual journey and its influence on her early work experiences.

> Chapter 3—*Developing Organizational Spiritual Leadership* introduces and explains the organizational spiritual leadership model and uses it to illustrate, through Lynne Sedgmore's mid-career experiences, how personal spiritual leadership provides the basis for organizational spiritual leadership development.

> Chapter 4—*CEL: Set Up, Disarray, and a New Beginning* uses the organizational spiritual leadership model to examine the early formation of CEL and the challenges Lynne Sedgmore initially faced as CEO.

> Chapter 5—*A Privileged Conversation: Democratizing Strategy through Spiritual Leadership* describes how Lynne Sedgmore used an executive coach and a renewed focus on her personal and organizational leadership to democratize strategy and create the context within which CEL as a spiritual organization could thrive.

> Chapter 6—*The Spirit at Work Award* explores the characteristics of CEL as an exemplar of personal and organizational spiritual leadership models that led to CEL receiving the prestigious International Spirit at Work Award.

> Chapter 7—*Spiritual Leadership in Action* reviews the research study of CEL and the tools it used to assess and implement the organizational spiritual leadership model.

> Chapter 8—*CEL: Maximizing the Triple Bottom Line through Spiritual Leadership* examines how CEL as a high performance organization began to imple-

ment the spiritual leadership balanced scorecard business model to maximize the triple bottom line.

Chapter 9—*The Legacy of CEL* covers the merger of CEL into a much larger organization, the loss of its identity as a spiritual organization, and the legacy and lessons it left for future organizations interested in maximizing the triple bottom line through spiritual leadership.

A Note about Narrative and Terms

We employ here language that is in common use in the discourse on spirituality, such as "altruistic love," "transcendence," "spiritual journey," "calling," and "dark night of the soul." We employ these terms either because they have been used by the subjects of this study, or because they are often found in the relevant practitioner and academic literature on spirituality. We do not infuse these terms with religious over- or under-tones. We do not advocate for any spirituality or faith. We simply aim to communicate in a language that is accessible and that imparts the "spirit" of our study.

1

The Beginning

Three Tribes Come Together to Turn Problems into Opportunity

In April 2004, Lynne Sedgmore became CEO of the Centre for Excellence in Leadership (CEL)—a fledgling organization in disarray. Her charge was to lead three tribes from North and South England to become a powerful force for leadership improvement and effectiveness across the learning and skills land.

These three tribes were:

1. *The Lancastrian Academic Heavies.* A highly respected and feared northern hills tribe, renowned for its leading edge research in leadership worldwide and its fierce guarding of its knowledge, reputation, and expertise.
2. *The Ashridge Business School Corporate Leadership Specialists,* who hailed from the hamlet of Berkhamsted and lived in a magnificent mansion in the Southern region. This tribe was charming

Spiritual Leadership in Action, pages 1–14
Copyright © 2013 by Information Age Publishing

1

and flexible, fiercely proud of its track record of adapting and responding to any customer need or request.

3. *The Learning and Skills Development Agency* (LSDA), *a Sector Specific Leadership Tribe*, based in the capital, London. They were a more humble, quiet tribe of people, open to learning from the other tribes, but they fiercely guarded their experience and knowledge of providing leadership in the Learning and Skills sector over many years, an experience and knowledge the other two tribes did not possess.

There were also five travelers from another dimension, the Governmental Department for Education and Skills (DFES), the planet of targets and bureaucracy: a planet filled with mountains of paper and millions of forms to fill in and boxes to check; a planet with masses of frenzy, activity, and measuring everything and everyone to their own exacting standards.

Lynne's task as CEO was to bring these tribes and travelers together in harmony, to generate a common vision and culture, to birth a singular organization, the Centre for Excellence in Leadership (CEL), and to deliver the best possible leadership development for leaders across the learning and skills land. Easy, she thought, as she had taken up new leadership roles many times before with new teams at various levels in different colleges. Yet this was different...

Early on in her professional career, Lynne envisioned leading an organization on spiritual principles. As her career advanced, Lynne focused on how to get the best out of a team and individuals. She observed how successful leaders listened to their staff, built good relationships, and gained mutual respect. She saw that, for her, competence was important, but she was more motivated by those who gave praise, encouragement, and genuinely thoughtful feedback to her actions, pointing out her mistakes as well as work done well. She felt alienated by managers who were self interested, used information as power, and generated fear as a means of getting things done.

Lynne started to read books on management and organizational development. She soon became convinced that the current management and leadership command and control paradigm to maximize investor and management wealth at the expense of employees and other key stakeholders was a flawed philosophy. Instead, she believed there is an inner longing in every person's heart for deep meaning, a higher purpose, and a desire for the infinite; and she felt compelled to make this a part of the way she led others.

In CEL, the three tribes and travelers all spoke different languages and different leadership pedagogies, and they saw the world in very different ways. They fought each other fiercely, however subtly, for territory and control. Each thought they knew the best and right way and struggled to respect and value the other tribes. Lynne soon realized that before she could bring unity to this organization, she must first find this unity in herself. It is this woman's inner unity—painfully and joyfully achieved through her personal spiritual journey and discussed in more detail in the next chapter—that created the possibility for a leadership that reconciles inner human development, sustainability, and economic success.

However, the UK public sector does not have a tradition of accepting and supporting overt spirituality in the workplace. Lynne recognized that any acceptance of leading from a spiritual perspective would only happen once CEL was firmly established as a highly effective organization. Therefore, the aim from the start was to be a high performing organization, to maximize the potential of everyone they touched, and to make a significant and positive impact on the learning and skills sector.

During the short five years of its existence, CEL demonstrated that a public sector organization can generate profits while simultaneously improving the lives of employees and key stakeholders. This vision became the core management philosophy of CEL to maximize, through conscious personal and organizational spiritual leadership, employee wellbeing and stakeholder satisfaction while increasing productivity and profitability—the triple bottom line of "people, planet, and profit."

Like Lynne, many leaders today are challenged to discover business models that accentuate and promote this triple bottom line (Fry & Nisiewicz, 2013). Understanding how to do this requires a knowledge of the synergistic effect of workplace spirituality and spiritual leadership on financial success. The spiritual leadership balanced scorecard business model, which draws from the fields of workplace spirituality, spiritual leadership, and conscious capitalism in order to maximize the triple bottom line, helps meet this challenge.

To start, this chapter will define workplace spirituality and introduce the model of organizational spirituality that CEL used to maximize the triple bottom line. Subsequent chapters will introduce models of personal and organizational spiritual leadership and detail how to maximize the triple bottom line through the balanced scorecard business model of spiritual leadership.

Organizational Spirituality

CEL was at the forefront of implementing organizational spirituality in the UK. In October 2007, CEL won the International Spirit at Work Award for its pioneering success in implementing spirituality in the workplace, its commitment to spiritual leadership, and its focus on reflective practice. CEL was the second UK organization, after the iconic Body Shop, to be honored with this prestigious international award for its work in creating a new paradigm for organizational performance, one that values wellbeing, social justice, spiritual development, and sustainability—in short, the whole person—as much as business output and material wealth.

In conjunction with the *Journal of Management, Spirituality and Religion* and its founding editor, Professor Yochanan Altman, CEL also jointly sponsored an in-depth research project and a series of workshops in the UK centered on organizational spirituality and facilitated the attendance of interested employees, customers, and partners. Professor Altman and his colleagues were commissioned to study organizational effectiveness and wellbeing in CEL through an in-depth examination of the organization as seen by its principal stakeholders (Altman, Ozbilgin, & Wilson, 2007). A specific objective of this study was to examine the spiritual essence of CEL as a non-faith-based organization striving to do good. The following section summarizes the findings that support the model of organizational spirituality.

Organizational Spirituality: Definitions

Workplace spirituality is a relatively new field of enquiry. The following definitions, however, were considered to be helpful in relation to organizational spirituality:

> Workplace spirituality is a framework of organizational values evidenced in the culture that promotes employees' experience of transcendence through the work process, facilitating their sense of being connected to others in a way that provides feelings of completeness and joy. (Giacalone & Jurkiewicz, 2003)

> Recognition of an inner life that nourishes and is nourished by meaningful work that takes place in the context of community. (Ashmos & Duchon, 2000)

Additionally, Jeff Pfeffer (2003), professor of organizational behavior at Stanford University, suggests that there are three spiritual elements valued by people at work:

- ▪ realizing their potential as persons,
- ▪ undertaking work with social value or social meaning, and
- ▪ feeling part of a large community or interconnected.

Based on the above, essential elements for workplace and organizational spirituality include support of employees' inner lives and a support that nourishes a sense of transcendence through meaningful work within a culture or community that facilitates a sense of connectedness and belonging.

Model of Organizational Spirituality

As part of this original research, a model of organizational spirituality was formulated against which CEL could be assessed (Altman, Ozbilgin, Wilson, 2007). Drawing on the above definitions, the model of organizational spirituality given in Figure 1.1 proposes that the spiritual organization has a virtuous cycle. It assumes that there is a critical mass of individuals with a spiritual orientation who join the organization (or who develop their spiri-

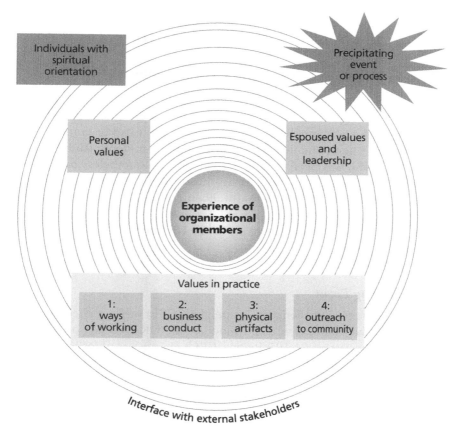

Figure 1.1 Model of organizational spirituality.

tuality through their work in the organization). A precipitating event or process can be discerned as a starting point that triggers the onset and pulls the organization toward organizational spirituality.

The experience of organizational members is the crucible of the organization's spiritual sense-making, informed by individuals and their personal values on the one hand, and by the espoused organizational values as manifested by its leadership on the other hand. In turn, members' experiences shape and are shaped by the organization's values in practice.

Values in practice (what the organization acts out) are manifested in different ways. There are ways of working, which may be observed (e.g., management styles), as well as business conduct that follows explicitly ethical standards and physical artifacts (such as the office layout). A further value in practice is outreach to the community (e.g., corporate social responsibility). In a spiritual organization, there will be congruence between espoused values and values in practice. Ways of working and business conduct will be manifested in the organization's interaction with external stakeholders.

CEL as a Model of Organizational Spirituality

CEL embodied the model of organizational spirituality given in Figure 1.1 by listening to customers, encouraging their feedback, and responding to their needs; this was mirrored internally through a strong emphasis on trust, empowerment, and delegation. Although the in-depth study did not suggest that CEL was perfect by any means, CEL nonetheless offered an impressive combination of spirituality-informed policy and spirituality-guided conduct for the benefit and wellbeing of its members, stakeholders, customers, and the community at large, which made it a trailblazer in the field of organizational spirituality in the UK and within the UK public sector in particular.

A Precipitating Event

The Centre for Excellence in Leadership (CEL) was launched in October 2003 as a key national agency funded by the UK Secretary of State for Skills within the *Success for All* initiative. CEL's charge was to foster and support leadership improvement, reform, and transformation throughout the learning and skills sector. This was the vocational education system funded by the UK government comprising over 600,000 staff, seven million learners, nearly 400 colleges, adult and community learning, and 2000 workplace training organizations. From then until October 2008, CEL served the existing and future leaders of all providers, including:

- further education (FE) colleges,
- work based learning (training and work-based learning providers),
- adult community learning providers,
- sixth form colleges,
- independent providers and specialist colleges,
- offender learning, and
- voluntary organizations.

In a series of interviews with CEL staff and stakeholders, interviewees described the turbulent birth of CEL, which, as described earlier, was originally conceived as a partnership. There appeared to be structural, philosophical, and pedagogic differences among the partners (tribes). While several respondents described CEL as a failing organization, others considered that it was dysfunctional and struggling, but not failing, as it continued to deliver leadership programs to clients. These early days were described as a bitter and negative experience by a number of CEL personnel. Of concern was the lack of in-depth knowledge shown by the partner agencies about the particular needs of the learning and skills sector. One associate reported that there was a prescriptive, top-down attitude towards the dissemination of leadership expertise. Three interviewees, who due to their position could afford a broader perspective, commented that these difficulties should be seen as inevitable teething problems at the starting phase of any organization.

This was the challenging scenario that confronted the new CEO, Lynne Sedgmore. Within one month after assuming her duties, CEL was issued a red alert audit, which was transformed to green within 12 months. This was achieved through "very, very hard work by the chief executive," according to one interviewee, and by her setting challenging targets.

With a new physical location, designed to have all employees in a singular space, new people joined, forming a critical mass, and the organization became what has been described as "CELish."

Individuals with Spiritual Orientation and Personal Values

Responses to a question about personal values included:

- treating people with respect;
- professionalism, do the best job for the sector;
- awareness, knowing what customers think and want;
- self-reflective about what is done well and what could be done better;
- honesty, integrity;

- principles around public service, value for money, good quality service;
- maintaining good relationships within CEL and in the sector;
- openness;
- hard working; and
- equality, including social inclusion.

Throughout the interviews, constant references to "the sector" were notable. The destination for CEL's activities, the learner (both concrete and abstract) within the learning and skills sector, appeared always present in the discussion. The following is a typical statement:

> I feel like [I am] contributing to the sector in a way which makes the community a better place and does something for the world.

The reference to both community and the world is significant. There was, however, a general avoidance of the spiritual and transcendent when asked about values, which mirrors documented observations about the reluctance of individuals to talk about faith in the workplace. Still, nearly 40% of respondents replied in the high affirmative to the question, "How much of your complete soul are you able to express at work?"

Several interviewees identified themselves as Christian, of different churches. There was a strictly observant Muslim and a Quaker. Many identified themselves as spiritual but not specifically religious. Three of the self-identified Christians were quite specific that their faith was accepted but not nurtured by their experience within or with CEL; their faith provided the bedrock for their values. Members of this group varied as to whether or not they would feel comfortable discussing their religious beliefs with colleagues. Of those identified as "spiritual," they referred to this spirituality in a number of ways, including: scope for goodness, a democratic and enabling approach, consciousness of power and energy, honesty, and caring.

Fewer than half the respondents felt "guided by a transcendental force in the midst of daily activities" and very few "prayed or meditated at work," though about half did outside work. CEL also had self-defined agnostics and atheists. All agreed that they were respected and acknowledged.

Espoused Values and Leadership

While the research was under way, a number of strategic forums took place, with the aim to rethink, redraw, and refine CEL's values. These were framed as follows:

- Learner focused—We empower and enable everyone we work with to achieve their full leadership potential;
- Professional—We are passionate, energetic, and dedicated professionals who deliver high standards and performance;
- Reflective—We are reflective practitioners continually improving our professionalism and seeking feedback;
- Collaborative—We are a partnership organization and believe in sharing our learning and expertise;
- Creative—We think outside the box and constantly seek innovative, new ways of seeing the world, and we strive constantly to learn and improve and create an open and supportive culture; and
- Diverse—We celebrate and respect our differences alongside ensuring inclusivity and equality of opportunity.

As the main proponent of organizational spirituality within CEL, CEO Lynne Sedgmore was reported as talking openly about soul and spirit. The degree of comfort with this type of talk varied among employees and stakeholders, some welcoming it, and others feeling uncomfortable, both about the idea of spirituality itself, and also because it [sometimes] conflicted with religious beliefs and ideological positions. One interviewee wondered whether some people might feel alienated. Another, acknowledging that CEL strove for recognition of the inner life and nourishing meaningful work, queried to what extent was that realistic, given the necessary focus on delivery.

Values in Practice

In terms of day-to-day practice, there were views that CEL both did and did not live up to its values, the former predominating. This is one example:

> CEL is such a good organization to work for. For the first time I have felt what it is like to be part of an organization that really does live out its values—putting into practice its philosophy on developing individuals, their creativity, and ability to work together as a team.

There were references also to integrity, transparency, accountability, and public sector values. One manager referred to "genuine love and respect for each other," although not always explicitly expressed. A newcomer commented that the culture of CEL was very positive, friendly, approachable, with staff wanting to make a difference.

Another temporary incumbent talked about the congruence between values and the general way CEL operated. Staff were very fired up and "all bought into the whole culture." The interviewee perceived this as being highly inculcated, top down, with a passion to do things right, and had never seen it before in "either private or public sector: it had only been a theory in a textbook."

However, there were comments that CEL did not always live up to its values. An associate thought that there was an inconsistent understanding of values throughout the organization and described sometimes really feeling part of a cohesive team, while at other times encountering attitudes that seemed defensive and territorial.

Employees criticized the induction of new staff, questioned senior managers' support for some roles, referred to non-permanent staff being excluded from bonus payments, and commented that despite commitment to spirituality and diversity, adequate facilities for private prayer (contemplation, meditation) were lacking.

The Experience of Organizational Members

High median ratings were achieved in response to statements such as "My work gives me a feeling of personal accomplishment," "The work I do is very important to me," and "I understand and am committed to my organization's vision." Many respondents valued the opportunity to be creative and innovative in their work, and allied to this was fun, not only on "away days" (there were informal outings, celebrations, and socializing outside work).

Ways of Working

Pressure of work meant that staff could find themselves working extra hours at short notice. It was noted that the chief executive and her deputy had a good work/life balance. Staff were allowed to work flexible hours, and from home.

Although expressing high levels of job satisfaction, managers perceived CEL to be more "stressed" (versus "relaxed") than non-managers did. Autonomy and delegation of authority were highly valued, and some expressed concern that with growth and streamlining of activities and procedures, some of that autonomy would be lost. It was clear from several interviewees that they considered policies and procedures to be underdeveloped, even counterproductive—for example, duplicate requests for statistics; too much last minute activity, such as responding to invitations to tender—so people became derailed from the task in hand. Yet, this lack of procedure was not always seen as a bad thing, as it encouraged creativity and innovation. A "can do" attitude prevailed.

Being different. A frequently discussed topic among interviewees was the difference between CEL and other organizations inside and outside the sector. It was described as responsive, quick, client-focused, risk taking, and delivering much more in comparison to other government agencies. An external stakeholder described contact with CEL as energizing, positive, and life enhancing, adding that it "can take your breath away."

Other descriptors used included refreshing, positive, passionate, enthusiastic, and challenging. For those coming from a more formal government setting, they appreciated levels of autonomy and discretion not previously experienced. Staff were described by a newcomer as motivated, driven, and focused. Others commented on the lack of an obvious hierarchy. Some staff described it as familial. For some, working at CEL was a liberating experience compared to previous work experiences.

Mistakes. A number of interviewees said that there was a no blame culture, providing people with a safe environment to take risks and innovate. One interviewee said: "I know if I messed up, I would not get into trouble."

Teamwork. Many positive comments were made about teamwork. There was broad agreement that CEL was one big team in the way it functioned, with everyone pulling in the same direction and people helping each other. Extending the team concept to off-site associates presented challenges though, and one manager commented on the need for wider team-building. There were references made to a "silo mentality," part of which seemed to be caused by a sense of urgency and lack of time.

Away days. One distinctive aspect of the CEL way of doing things was the "away days" framework; everyone who talked about these did so with enthusiasm. Organized by HR and held for two days, twice each year, these were designed to offer developmental opportunities for junior staff, who were in charge of program content and had responsibility for budget.

"Away days" were an umbrella framework for CEL and all its constituents—full-time and part-time, core and associates, external contractors and long-term affiliates—to participate in a community "happening" of learning in a comfortable environment, enjoying each other's company, and having fun. They also offered an opportunity to address organizational topical issues (and for considered reflection) and to facilitate learning. One observer thought it was a way of "...feeling part of a larger community...interconnecting."

Business Conduct

Respondents reported favorably on CEL's leadership and its diversity initiatives.

Leadership. Leadership was CEL's raison d'être. As a leadership development agency, the conduct of its leaders was of considerable relevance. A number of respondents indicated that CEL had developed a model of spiritual leadership, which the chief executive encouraged from the top. A new appointee found it very positive to be told: "This is a high-delegation, high-trust environment—off you go."

Responses to the open-ended questions in the spiritual leadership questionnaire, whose quantitative results are covered in detail in Chapter 7, were complimentary to CEL's leadership team. The chief executive was described as someone who was very supportive, gave people responsibility, acted as a great figurehead, had high professional credibility, demonstrated high energy, and communicated success well internally.

Diversity. A particular focus for CEL was diversity, both in relation to its own staff and to its role for the learning and skills sector. CEL was visibly diverse in relation to nationality and ethnic background, skills and experience, as well as age and sexuality. There was a majority of women throughout the organization at all levels. This spread of diversity is unusual in both the private and public sector in the UK. CEL was recognized as particularly strong in this area by the Department for Education and Skills (DFES). Here are some examples of how CEL actively modeled diversity for the sector.

To address disadvantage within the sector, CEL offered a specialist program, First Steps to Leadership, for Black and ethnic minority potential managers, which was described as "a phenomenal success." The aim was to roll this out to other groups, customizing it for women and people with disabilities, for instance. CEL achieved a place in the top 50 Stonewall diversity champions as a gay friendly workplace and won the British Diversity Award through the work of its Black Leadership Initiative.

Diversity awareness training was mandatory for all staff, who were also encouraged to have individual coaching and take part in a voluntary program of exploring the Enneagram, self reflective tools, and Dignity at Work training days. Observance of faith disciplines was respected and facilitated.

CEL's Faith Communities Toolkit, developed for clients and freely available to all staff, provided a valuable faith literacy guide to a multiplicity of religious and spiritual approaches and belief systems, making it clear that CEL had no particular religious or spiritual affiliation.

CEL also sponsored a study into perceptions of faith and spirituality in FE colleges and published the report *Making space for faith: Values, beliefs and faiths in the learning and skills sector.*

Physical Artifacts

The physical layout also supported CEL's commitment to being a spiritual organization.

Office layout. Staff were based in one large, open-plan office. Some appreciated the egalitarian message that this arrangement conveyed and liked the opportunities for frequent face-to-face contact, while others heartily disliked the lack of personal space and hot-desking arrangements and found it noisy and distracting. It was also stressful working next to the enquiry line or an unanswered telephone. In a focus group, it was said that you could sometimes feel the politics, atmosphere, and stress of the main office.

Dress. The conformity of outward outlook that becomes the norm in many organizations was not evident in CEL. Modes of dress included conventionally dressed men (there is usually less variation among men than women); women dressed in smart casual style of tailored trousers and shirts; jeans, spiky hair and body piercing; and full-length skirt and hijab.

Outreach to the Community and External Stakeholders

Statistics about the take-up of courses indicated a good relationship with customers. There was evidence of good feedback, especially from colleges.

Initially there was no formal outreach work undertaken by CEL, although individuals had been supported by colleagues in charitable fun runs and other fundraising activities. As a result of the research project, all staff were allowed three paid days a year to work in a charity of their choice. This opportunity had enthusiastic take-up.

Conclusion

In this chapter we provided an initial introduction and general overview of the Centre for Excellence in Leadership and its CEO, Lynne Sedgmore. Then we introduced a model of organizational spirituality that provides the context for subsequent discussion of the personal and organizational spiritual leadership models and the spiritual leadership balanced scorecard business model. The rest of the book will focus on further describing CEL, its evolution as a spiritual organization, and how CEO Lynne Sedgmore and the CEL board and colleagues implemented and put these models into practice.

Practical Tools

For those interested in implementing spiritual leadership to maximize the triple bottom line, the major tools introduced in this chapter include:

1. *Definition of workplace spirituality*—Identifies the key elements for organizational spirituality.
2. *The model of organizational spirituality*—Provides the broader organizational context and necessary components for implementing personal and organizational spiritual leadership and the spiritual leadership balanced scorecard business model.

2

The Journey of Personal Spiritual Leadership

CEL's CEO, Lynne Sedgmore

For Lynne Sedgmore, the Centre for Excellence in Leadership (CEL) was the culmination of a lifelong spiritual journey: a deep inquiry into how she could integrate her spirituality, professional, and organizational life. Her work in further education has been a true and well loved professional vocation since 1982 and a place of spiritual integration and growth since 1989. Over the years she has come to the realization that "work is worship" and the place where she manifests her love of and service to others. As her career progressed, she became certain that there is an inner longing in every person's heart for meaning and purpose and ultimately for the transcendent, however buried or unconscious that may be for some. This knowing compelled her to want to make a difference in the way she led others. Like many of her colleagues she spent a considerable amount of time in the workplace, and she felt that the workplace was for many their primary community outside the family.

Spiritual Leadership in Action, pages 15–32
Copyright © 2013 by Information Age Publishing

After working for 22 years in various positions in further education (FE) colleges, Lynne became CEO of CEL. She was convinced that she could improve the lives of her employees and the FE leadership community while at the same time making a profit so that they could do more and more good work—seeped in abundance. Through her commitment to her spiritual journey, she constantly sought to transcend her selfish ego through a regular spiritual practice so that she could better love and serve others. Lynne also wanted her personal spiritual journey to manifest itself through organizational spiritual leadership by engaging organizational members through hope and faith in a vision of service to key stakeholders based on the values of altruistic love. That initial vision has since become the core of her management and leadership philosophy: to draw on her personal spiritual leadership to co-create sustainable and healthy organizations that promote employee wellbeing and social responsibility along with improving productivity and profitability—the triple bottom line.

There's a saying that you can't lead others if you can't lead yourself. To do so requires strong personal leadership. Personal leadership is the self-confident ability to crystallize your thinking and establish a clear direction for your life, to commit yourself to moving in that direction, and then to take determined action to acquire, accomplish, or become whatever you identify as the ultimate goal for your life. For Lynne it was the goal of enlightenment or, as Eckhardt Tolle in *The Power of Now* (2004) describes it, a felt oneness with Being to be found by abiding in a state of "feeling-realization" where you are present moment-to-moment and your attention is fully and intensely in the now.

Personal leadership is a process of developing a positive self-identity that gives you the courage and self-confidence necessary to consciously choose actions that satisfy your needs, enable you to persevere, and allow you to accept responsibility for the outcome. Doing what you know is right and productive for you regardless of obstacles or the opinions of others is the essence of personal leadership. To apply strong personal leadership, leaders must recognize and believe in their own untapped potential, develop a strong self-identity, be self-motivated through hope and faith in their personal vision, and define success in terms of the progressive realization of worthwhile predetermined personal goals.

Personal spiritual leadership recognizes that there is a spiritual element to personal leadership. Leaders cannot implement workplace spirituality and the model of organizational spirituality without personal spiritual leadership. In this chapter we first discuss the personal spiritual leadership model and the qualities of personal spiritual leadership. Then we describe the essence of the spiritual journey and its role in developing the qualities of personal spiritual leadership. Finally, CEL's CEO Lynne Sedgmore's early life and career history is offered as a case study of one person's spiritual journey and how she worked to develop the qualities of personal spiritual leadership.

The Personal Spiritual Leadership Model

Personal spiritual leadership, as illustrated by Figure 2.1, requires not only the exercise of strong personal leadership but also an inner life practice that supports hope/faith in a vision of serving others through altruistic love. By being committed to a vision of service to others, one has a sense of calling in that he or she makes a difference in other peoples' lives and, therefore, life has meaning and purpose. In authentically living the values of altruistic love through the care, concern, and appreciation of both one's self and others, one experiences membership and has a sense of being understood and appreciated. Calling and membership are two key aspects of spiritual wellbeing, which is the source of the individual outcomes of personal spiritual leadership—personal commitment and productivity, positive human health, psychological well-being, and life satisfaction. These outcomes generate spontaneous, cooperative effort and enhance one's ability to learn, develop, and use one's skills and knowledge to benefit self and others, family, community, and any organization one chooses to join.

Inner Life

Developing personal spiritual leadership requires an understanding of the spiritual journey—a journey of transformation to become less ego-centered and more other-centered in striving to fulfill one's ultimate purpose

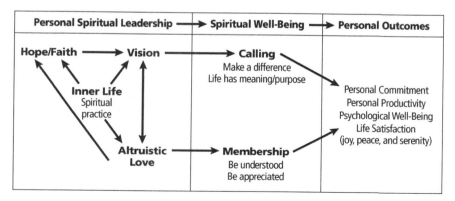

Figure 2.1 Personal spiritual leadership.

through love and service of others. This means cultivating an inner life practice (e.g., spending time in nature, prayer, meditation, reading inspirational literature, yoga, observing religious traditions, writing in a journal) that provides the foundation for a vision of loving and serving others. It also requires a supportive spiritual community and perhaps working with a spiritual coach or director. Both are important to provide regular feedback and counsel concerning the motives of any proposed action. This is to guard against spiritual pride where apparent service to others is in reality about satisfying the ego's own selfish needs and desires.

Inner life and transcendence. At the heart of inner life is people's quest to step beyond their self-interest and connect to and serve something greater than themselves. The connection to something greater can include being a member of and serving in an organization that has a mission that provides the individual with a sense of purpose. Moreover, if one so believes, this connection to something greater can include an ultimate, sacred, and divine force or deity. This connection can provide people with purpose and meaning, a values system based on loving kindness, a set of rules to live by to achieve wellbeing, and a source of strength and comfort during times of adversity.

Transcendence is important to personal spiritual leadership development because it allows one to step outside, or beyond, ego-centered interests to love and serve others more selflessly. Connecting to and serving an ultimate, a sacred, and divine or higher power or deity can provide leaders and followers with a sense of purpose and meaning and influence their leadership philosophies. This connection can influence leaders' values system, beliefs about truths in the world, and how to find meaning and purpose. Most faiths and philosophies value and encourage service to others as a means of finding meaning, purpose, and wellbeing. This connection has the potential to influence leaders' perceptions of themselves, what they attend to, how they perceive situations, and their behavior.

Another major purpose of an inner life practice in personal spiritual leadership is to gain awareness and, ultimately, to abide in a state of self-actualization, which is often termed self-realization or enlightenment. Enlightenment is simply a natural state of felt oneness with the universe that holds all of experience in an open, accepting way. To be enlightened means to be in the now. It is an awakening moment-by-moment to the nature of life and death, accepting reality as it is rather than how you want it to be. This awareness is a sense of connectedness with something greater than oneself that is universal and infinite, and, if one so believes, an ultimate, sacred, and divine force, Being, or God.

Lynne says she cannot remember a time when she was not asking spiritual/religious questions, nor could she imagine her life without such focus and exploration. Over the years, her view of the role spirituality and religion play in her life has changed and refined as her spirituality has grown and developed. Today she says her relationship to transcendence is a broad inclusive and direct experience of spirituality and cannot be confined to one tradition or approach, as she is passionate about exploring all paths and approaches to spiritual growth and expression.

As CEL's CEO, Lynne Sedgmore tended not to use the word God; instead she preferred expressions such as transcendence, higher power, universe, essence, and so on. These are more neutral words that, in her experience, create less adverse reactions or defensiveness from other people who have had a negative experience with formalized religion. She remembers a time when it was hard for her to use the "God word," as it had negative connotations with the traditional and limited concept of the "fire and brimstone" Christian God whose purpose was to catalogue one's sins and damn the sinner to hell. Moreover, she never wanted to provoke unnecessary reactions in others who may be struggling with the word themselves and letting it get in the way of good dialogue.

Inner life and mindfulness. Mindfulness is the English equivalent of the Pali words *sati* and *sampajana,* which are translated as awareness, circumspection, discernment, and retention. It means to pay attention or awaken to what is occurring in one's immediate experience with care and discernment. Mindfulness entails becoming aware and conscious, in an open, nonjudgmental manner, of one's moment-to-moment experiences, whether thoughts, feelings, body sensations, needs, wants, and motivations behind behavior. It is the knowing of one's experience as it is being experienced: knowing one's state of mind (thoughts) and emotions (feelings) without judging, evaluating, or trying to change them. Mindfulness is essential for inner life and development of character because it allows for one to be in touch with subtle feelings and intuitions that can result in better understanding of, and ability to exercise greater control in response to, situations and challenges as they arise in the now moment.

Mindfulness is a key part of the spiritual journey; it invites one to take responsibility for being human and to open to the unconscious biases that are influencing decisions and relationships. It helps to develop spiritual self-awareness of one's values and attitudes and the ability to monitor one's thoughts and emotions (also know as meta-cognition). Without mindfulness, one is not aware that events, people, or our plans to control the future are dominating consciousness and inhibiting development of the components of one's character for personal spiritual leadership.

Lynne reports an unquenchable thirst for exploring and developing her inner life and mindfulness through meditation and says she cannot live without daily contemplation and spiritual practices. She has experimented with a wide range of approaches to physical, psychological, emotional, and spiritual awareness, plus several mindfulness schools and traditions, to realize her wish to go deeper and deeper in all facets of her being.

Spiritual Leadership

Spiritual leadership, with inner life as its source, emerges from the interaction of hope/faith, vision, and altruistic love. The qualities of personal spiritual leadership are shown in Table 2.1.

Vision. Vision refers to a picture of the future with some implicit or explicit commentary on why people should strive to create that future. In order to motivate change, visions serve three important functions: clarifying the general direction of change, simplifying hundreds or thousands of more detailed decisions, and helping to quickly and efficiently coordinate the actions for oneself or group members. A vision defines the journey and why the leaders and followers are taking it. It energizes, gives meaning to work, garners commitment, and establishes a standard of excellence. An effective vision has broad appeal, defines the destination and journey, reflects high ideals, and encourages hope and faith.

Hope/Faith. Hope/faith is also the source for the conviction that the vision, either personal or organizational, will be fulfilled. Hope is a desire with expectation of fulfillment. Faith adds certainty to hope. Taken together, hope/faith is a firm belief in something for which there is no evidence.

TABLE 2.1 Qualities of Personal Spiritual Leadership

Vision	Altruistic Love	Hope/Faith
• Broad Appeal to Key Stakeholders • Defines the Destination and Journey Reflects High Ideals • Encourages Hope/Faith • Establishes Standard of Excellence	• Trust/Loyalty • Forgiveness/Acceptance/ Gratitude • Integrity • Honesty • Courage • Humility • Kindness • Compassion • Patience/Meekness/ Endurance • Fun	• Endurance • Perseverance • Do What It Takes • Stretch Goals • Expectation of Reward/ Victory • Excellence

It is based on values, attitudes, and behaviors that demonstrate absolute certainty and trust that what is desired and expected will come to pass. Individuals with hope/faith have a vision of where they are going and how to get there. They are willing to face opposition and endure hardships and suffering in order to achieve their goals. Hope/faith is demonstrated through effort, action, or work. In action hope/faith is like a race that has two essential components—the victory (vision) and the joy of preparing for the race itself. Both components are necessary and essential elements of hope/faith to generate the necessary effort to pursue the vision.

Altruistic Love. For spiritual leadership, altruistic love is defined as "a sense of wholeness, harmony, and wellbeing produced through care, concern, and appreciation for both self and others" (Fry, 2008). There are great emotional and psychological benefits from separating love, or care and concern for others, from need, which is the essence of giving to and serving others unconditionally. The fields of medicine and positive psychology have begun to study and confirm that love has the power to overcome the negative influence of destructive emotions such as resentment, worry, fear, and anger. Underlying this definition are the values of integrity, patience, kindness, forgiveness, humility, selflessness, trust, loyalty, and truthfulness. Altruistic love defines the set of key values, assumptions, understandings, and ways of thinking considered to be morally right. Spiritual leaders embody and abide in these values through their everyday attitudes and behavior.

Spiritual Wellbeing

The emergence of spiritual leadership then taps into the fundamental needs of both leader and followers for spiritual wellbeing by positively enhancing their sense of calling and membership. Calling or being called (vocationally) gives a sense of making a difference in the lives of others. Membership gives a sense of belonging or community. These two elements of spiritual wellbeing are universal and interconnected human needs.

Calling. Calling refers to how one makes a difference through service to others and, in doing so, finds meaning and purpose in life. Many people seek not only competence and mastery to realize their full potential through their work, but also a sense that work has some social meaning or value. The term calling has long been used as one of the defining characteristics of a professional. Professionals in general have expertise in a specialized body of knowledge. They have ethics centered on selfless service to clients/customers, an obligation to maintain quality standards within the profession, a commitment to their vocational field, a dedication to their work, and a strong commitment to their careers. Professionals believe their chosen profession is valuable, even essential to society, and they are proud to be a member of it. The need for calling is satisfied through both personal and organizational spiritual leadership.

Membership. Membership includes a sense of belonging and community: the cultural and social structures we are immersed in and through which we seek what William James, the founder of modern psychology, called man's most fundamental need—to be understood and appreciated. Having a sense of membership is a matter of interrelationships and connection through social interaction. Individuals value their affiliations, being interconnected, and feeling part of a larger community. As we devote ourselves to social groups, membership meshes us in a network of social connections that go as far as the group has influence and power and backwards and forwards in relation to its history.

Spiritual wellbeing, however, is not obtained by striving for it directly. One cannot experience a sense of spiritual wellbeing through calling and membership by trying to manufacture it. It is not produced when a leader focuses on monetary or other extrinsic goals, but instead occurs when leaders first establish a healthy workplace culture grounded in altruistic values and a transcendent vision.

Personal Outcomes

Personal spiritual leadership requires an inner life practice that is the source of hope/faith in a transcendent vision and personal values based on altruistic love. By committing to a vision of service to our key stakeholders, we discover a calling to make a difference in other people's lives, and, therefore, our lives have meaning and purpose. In living the values of altruistic love through the care, concern, and appreciation of both one's self and others, we experience membership and the sense of being understood and appreciated. The combined experiences of calling and membership are the essence of spiritual wellbeing, which is the source of the individual outcomes of personal spiritual leadership—personal commitment and productivity, positive human health, psychological wellbeing, and life satisfaction.

The Spiritual Journey

According to Father Thomas Keating (1999), a pioneer in the development of contemplative prayer, we all enter this world with three essential biological needs: security and survival, power and control, affection and esteem. We will not survive infancy if these biological needs are not adequately fulfilled. Then, in later childhood years, most of us are taught that happiness is to be found through identifying with and meeting the expectations of one's particular family, community group, or culture via the universal influence of cultural conditioning.

The energy that we put into trying to find happiness in fulfilling these emotional programs and cultural expectations tends to increase with time. This means placing the source of happiness in external relationships, which often leads to a sense of being dominated by external events and our emotional reactions to them. These daily events often frustrate our emotional programs for happiness, which gives rise to the destructive emotions of anger, resentment, worry, and fear. Much of this is rooted in the unconscious and is the cause of a pervasive illness that Keating calls the "universal human condition," which is deeply rooted and from which, according to Keating, we all suffer. In this condition, individuals find themselves in the midst of an intense emotional dialogue as well as emotional turmoil. This can become an ongoing cycle that is the source of much misery.

If one experiences these destructive emotions intensely and repeatedly, it is a sign that, either consciously or unconsciously, there is an expectation based on an emotional program for happiness or cultural conditioning that has been frustrated. In this sense one feels powerless over these events and emotions and that one's life is unmanageable. One may be able to lead what appears to be a relatively normal life, but there is no experience of true happiness.

The more one realizes that one's lives is unmanageable in this sense, the more one becomes open to undertake the spiritual journey (Benefiel, 2005, 2008). At this point one is willing to seek and explore the emotional programs for happiness and cultural conditioning that are the source of the unhappiness. In doing so one begins to discover a spiritual path that brings an added dimension to life in terms of joy, peace, and serenity. However, after a time the spiritual sojourner discovers these abundant spiritual gifts begin to disappear. This brings confusion and a sense of distance as the prayers that once brought bounty remain unanswered. After redoubling their efforts and only experiencing more dryness, many give up the spiritual quest at this point. Some spiritual and religious traditions refer to this point as the "first dark night of the soul."

Those who persevere on the spiritual journey emerge from this first dark night. They reach a point where they learn that the spiritual journey is really about their own transformation. Instead of praying and talking to a higher power or God asking for what they need, they discover the need to enter silence and listen more. This stage marks the beginning of a striving to transcend one's self-centered ego and become more other-centered through loving and serving others. Sojourners at this stage do not succumb to discouragement as readily. A habit develops to love and serve their neighbors and those in need despite their defects.

Those who continue may enter the "second dark night of the soul." In this place not only does prayer no longer work, but even their higher power appears to have disappeared. This seems true even as one lets go of old forms of prayer and becomes more open to listening for something new. There is a sense of being blocked with no new paths opening no matter how much effort is exerted. It is at this point that one learns to simply desire to be with the higher power or seek a sense of oneness with the universe, not looking for what it can give. This is hard to understand, especially if the seeker's true desire is his or her own transformation. However, many spiritual and religious traditions emphasize that this higher power is still working in hidden ways during this second dark night.

Ultimately if one perseveres, the second dark night yields to an emerging sense of oneness with all things, and the hidden work that occurred during the second dark night is revealed. This is the point at which one's ego and life become dedicated to a higher good. By far, most spiritual seekers glimpse this place and live in it briefly, then slip into a more ego-centered place. It is rare for one to arrive and stay at this unitive or nondual stage for long. But over time as they continue to walk the spiritual path, leaders can learn through an inner life based in mindfulness to live more and more fully in this place of letting go. This is what twelve step programs mean when they say the program is about "spiritual progress, not spiritual perfection."

To the extent leaders are able to undertake and live the spiritual journey, they are more dedicated to the higher good and available to the needs of the people they serve. Because their egos are more other-centered, these leaders can use their skills and energies to serve the good of the organization and society as a whole, rather than their own selfish interests.

I was born into an agnostic family. My mother had three miscarriages, and her first born child died in her arms at eight months in a totally unexpected tragedy. By the time she was pregnant with me she struggled with her belief and faith in a God of any kind. (I was born next, eight months after the death of my older sister). Alongside my younger sister Susan and brother Andrew, we attended Sunday school, more as a social norm than any religious requirement. One thing we always knew was that we were well loved and the center of our parents' universe, supported by the strong local working class community in which we grew up. Ours was a low income, working class family, close knit, and proud. Dad was a good provider, and Mum always used to say we may be poor, but we had no debts and were clean—you could have eaten off her floors. Education was seen as the way out for their children to have a better life, and we were given every support. To this day I visit my primary school every year with my mother to give out an award in my late dad's name to acknowledge the support they provided for us.

I am familiar with the ongoing debate as to whether leaders are born or made and have thought long and hard about it. In my own case it feels that it is a mixture of both. I recall as a child of six organizing the games in the street and with my friends, easily and naturally. I just seemed to know how to get the best from group situations. At my local primary school I was school prefect, and in grammar school I was elected chair of the sixth form society, was form charity monitor, and on five sports teams representing the school. But I was also a rebel (without a cause, yet) with a low boredom threshold and frequently in trouble. I had to learn the hard way to manage the boundary of keeping staff happy with good academic results while being able to enjoy school my way.

From the age of 10 I voluntarily attended local churches as I felt drawn deeply to "finding God" and was challenging church leaders on their lack of congruence with Jesus' teachings compared to how they were behaving. I found myself engaging the local Methodist Church, Church of England, and the Salvation Army in a deep desire to belong to a religious community.

The First Dark Night of the Soul. At 15 I experienced my "first dark night of the soul" through a deep emotional crisis of meaninglessness and a deep feeling that the material world was not for me. Seemingly, I could not find people or places to express what I needed spiritually, to find an inner sense of purpose and connection. Feeling spiritually alone and isolated, I felt I could not cope living a life that was so mundane and lacked something deeper, and I attempted suicide during an overwhelming period of meaninglessness and a loss of will to continue. I recall just wishing to go home to God. Luckily I was found shortly after taking an overdose, rushed to hospital, and then referred to a psychiatrist. With no obvious problems, such as pregnancy, school troubles, or family difficulties, the psychiatrist concluded that I was "just a silly child wanting attention," admonishing me to "grow up and get on with life."

At the time I had no words to explain what I know now, following therapy and deep reflection, was a spiritual crisis, with no one to turn to for spiritual guidance, understanding, and integration. Traumatized by the failure of everyone around me to understand my experience and by my inability to explain what was happening to me, I decided to give up on God and live life "their way," accepting the material world as it is and moving forward without a relationship with my God.

When I was 16, a nun came to speak at school, and she moved me profoundly as I sensed her inner peace and serenity. When I told my parents I wanted to visit the convent, they refused, as they thought my "God stuff" was getting out of hand and was probably the cause of my crisis the previous year. Being too weary to fight them, I did not go. However, since then I have had a deep fascination with monastic life and reverence for nuns and monks. I sometimes wonder how different my life would have been had I found a community of sympathetic mystical nuns at 16 . . .

From 17 to 18 I became a Mormon in a last ditch attempt to find a Christian community but soon left them due to their restrictive teachings on women and family. My parents were strongly opposed to my connection with the Mormons, and it caused terrible arguments as they were convinced I had some form of religious mania. At this point I gave up on God and religion, as it all felt so hard and conflicting, and since I could not find a true or comfortable place in any church.

The years from 17 to 26 saw my first dark night of the soul persist as I decided that Christianity was deeply problematic because the Church had so many flaws and could not accommodate the experiences and feelings I had. During this period I read the works of various writers on spirituality, while leading a normal young woman's life. I fell in love with my future husband at 18, married at 19, and gave birth to my daughter Keri at 20. Having a baby so young enabled me to experience total unconditional love and the power of placing another life before my own. This in itself was a spiritual experience and deeply fulfilling. Yet as a working class girl supported by my poor family to get a university education, I was determined also to get my degree and not let my family down, whilst remaining active in cultural activities and becoming involved in left-of-center and feminist politics.

Emergence from the First Dark Night. Despite a happy, active, and productive life, deep down inside me something was always missing. Engaging in the material world and experiencing academic, political, and familial success was not enough. In 1983, aged 26, I accepted that I missed exploring my spirituality and returned to a conscious spiritual search, beginning to explore the Buddhist path. This path felt more open and inclusive than Christianity and made me think about spirituality in a non-theistic way.

To nourish my soul and spirit, I spent whatever time I could in retreat environments and in personal growth workshops, examining many spiritual gurus but never really committing to a particular one. I was more interested in exploring all the faith, mystical, and spiritual traditions of the world, which led someone to describe me during this period as "religiously promiscuous." I found it to be a shrewd and apt comment and took no offense.

I sensed that somehow these spiritual explorations influenced my effectiveness in my professional life and that the two were powerfully interrelated. I felt that the more self aware I was becoming, the more effective I was at work. However, without role models, a relevant literature, nor other individuals with whom to share this understanding, it remained an undeveloped intuitive afterthought. It was during this period that I started my first full time job as a lecturer in 1982 in a further education (FE) college. I gained rapid promotion from a base grade lecturer, to lecturer two, to senior lecturer, to head of a department—three major promotions in two years was very unusual at that time for anyone, let alone a young woman. My progress continued with three department head roles from 1984 to 1989, including dean of Croydon Business School.

Eventually I was to discover that my true calling would be transforming the lives of students and staff for the better through FE. However, the environment in which I worked did not encourage the sharing of religion or spirituality in the workplace. As a lecturer and leader in FE and the public sector, sharing of personal growth experiences and religious beliefs was frowned upon and seen as inappropriate. Consequently I kept my personal and spiritual life private and separate from my work life. In addition to this, many of my colleagues and friends were not religious or overtly spiritual, and they tended to accept this part of me as "quirky."

In 1984 I attended my first Buddhist retreat and began attending a weekly meditation class and study group. On this retreat in a puja ceremony and meditation, I experienced an overwhelming feeling of metta bahavna—the Buddhist term for loving kindness. It made me cry as I felt connected with the whole universe and everyone within it. The depth of this first mystical experience has never left me. But I also felt overwhelmed since it was so powerful and difficult to contain, something I had to learn to do over the coming years.

I persevered and reached a point where I realized that the spiritual journey was really about my own transformation, beyond searching for a God out there and answers beyond myself. I discovered the need to enter silence and to meditate and to listen more. This marked another beginning of striving to transcend my self-centered ego and to become more other-centered through loving and serving others.

The Second Dark Night of the Soul. However, the second dark night was soon to follow. Within this "high flying" career I experienced a significant professional failure in Hackney College, London, where I was promoted into a head of department role from 1984 to 1986. Here I discovered that my usual approach, successful in Croydon College, was not working. I realized that I may have been promoted beyond my capability into a very difficult organization, and the repercussions were catching up with me. As part of this experience I became aware of the importance of the culture fit and common values between the individual and the organization. This professional failure affected me so severely that I went into serious weekly therapy to understand what was happening and to cope more effectively. I began also an even deeper spiritual inner journey from 1985 to 1989 with more concentrated meditation and further exploration of the Buddhist spiritual tradition and its insights.

I felt fragmented and knew that I needed to work even more deeply on myself to move forward across the emotional, psychological, and spiritual parts of my psyche that were not yet integrated. All sorts of difficult things were manifesting—my marriage was in trouble, my daughter was being bullied in school, I had a nasty car crash, and my mother-in-law was diagnosed with terminal cancer. Everything felt in flux and crisis. I knew I needed professional help and found it with a Jungian, integral therapist. It was a difficult time but also provided space for a new beginning. I found myself highly motivated about getting "fit" in every aspect of my being. I started meditation in earnest and joined a women's Buddhist study group. I discovered that although the therapy and meditation side by side had a beneficial impact almost immediately, it was also a long and painful exploration and journey to a fully integrated health and wholeness. I now began to experiment with new concepts of and words for God, such as universal spirit, the void, the transcendent, the divine, and higher power.

In this second dark night period, prayer no longer seemed to work, and even God seemed to have disappeared, leaving me empty and flat. I had a sense of being blocked with no new paths opening to the transcendent no matter how much effort I exerted. I simply desired to be with and to experience God, oneness, or the void for its own sake—not just for what the transcendent could do for me in the external world.

I found this phase of life hard to understand, especially since my true desire was my own transformation into a life of service and deep spiritual commitment. However, Buddhist training taught me, as do all religious traditions, that spirit is still working in hidden ways. Persevering, this second dark night gradually yielded to an emerging sense of Oneness, and the hidden work that I believe had occurred during this second dark night was revealed. At last I began to have deeper and more sustained experiences of union with the transcendent, experienced very differently now in oneness, as the nondual.

I had a powerful new level of spiritual experience in 1988 when attending a conference on spirituality in the workplace at Lancaster University. It happened in a lecture theatre while with others. I found my hands lifting as I was flooded with light into my head and hands. It felt wonderful, as if I was glowing all over from within and without. The person sitting next to me asked what had happened; she did not see the light but told me she could feel that something unusual was happening to me. When I came home, every time I meditated more light flowed, particularly in and from my hands, and I became certain that my path was to become a spiritual healer, as I knew that this light was not just for me but was for others too. I noted in my journal that April 7th, 1988 was a day of spiritual rebirth and that I would begin a new spiritually focused life. Alas, there was no-one in my life who had had similar experiences, although a close friend listened sympathetically.

Things moved on. In 1989 my marriage was dissolved amicably; we parted for various reasons, including our different views on spirituality. While supportive, my husband could not understand my constant searching for God, as he himself was a confirmed atheist, and I wanted a fellow traveler on the spiritual path. The same year, in March, I was appointed dean of Croydon Business School to take up the post in September. For the first time in my life I decided to take a month long vacation in July and traveled to the Skyros Centre in Greece, where I planned to rest, recuperate, and focus on my meditation practice and emotional state. It was here that I discovered a group of like minded people who have remained friends and soul companions for many years. Skyros turned out to be exactly what I needed at the time to support my spiritual realization, growth, and spiritual development. While there I had more nondual experiences that deeply influenced my future direction, values, and commitment to integrating spirituality into my whole life, including my workplace. I also revisited Christianity, the religion of my childhood and culture, and began a journey of healing all wounds and negative experience with churches and Christian beliefs.

While the desire to leave organizational life surfaced strongly throughout the next five years, I never really felt I could leave the FE system. I loved my professional work in FE colleges and never tired or lost enthusiasm for the job, however difficult and taxing it may have been at times. It was during this period that I really understood that work could be worship and how important being of service was to me. In Buddhist terms I began to understand that for me FE was "right livelihood" and how much I loved supporting and empowering FE students and staff.

Lynne Sedgmore's Early Journey of Personal Spiritual Leadership

Here we offer, in her own word's, a recounting of Lynne Sedgmore's early life and spiritual journey:

Lynne Sedgmore's early life and career experiences are an illustration of the challenges one faces in developing the qualities of personal spiritual leadership after committing to the spiritual journey—a journey of transformation to become less ego-centered in striving to fulfill one's ultimate purpose through love and service of others. Through her early childhood experiences and sense of emptiness that led to her "first dark night of the soul," Lynne found the honesty, open-mindedness, and willingness to undertake this journey, which ultimately led to exploring her emotional programs for happiness and cultural conditioning developed in early childhood.

However, this only happened when she exhausted her own resources and discovered that she could not alleviate her suffering or achieve happiness through the exercise of self-will alone. Lynne then began to cultivate an inner life practice to develop mindful awareness. She also sought a supportive spiritual community and sometimes worked with a spiritual guide or director to provide regular feedback and counsel concerning the motives of any proposed action. These practices were an essential source of strength that helped her through her early career "second dark night of the soul."

These experiences and spiritual practices were also essential for developing the qualities of hope/faith, vision, and altruistic love in personal spiritual leadership. In seeking a vision of service of others in her beloved further education sector, Lynne began to get a sense of spiritual wellbeing through calling and membership. Through calling she began to experience that she made a difference in other people's lives and, therefore, her life had meaning and purpose. In doing her best to live the values of altruistic love through the care, concern, and appreciation of both herself and others, she began to experience membership and the sense of being understood and appreciated. Through her increased spiritual wellbeing, Lynne increasingly realized the outcomes of personal spiritual leadership—higher levels of personal commitment and productivity, psychological wellbeing, and life satisfaction.

Conclusion

Developing personal spiritual leadership requires an understanding of the spiritual journey. It requires also finding the honesty, open-mindedness, and willingness to undertake the journey, leading ultimately to exploring our often crippling emotional programs for happiness and cultural conditioning. As part of this pilgrimage, one must change in fundamental ways. This change is based in the realization that, to the extent we can come to see others differently, we can undergo a profound personal transformation that can free us from anguished thoughts, and emotions. This entails a change of values and attitudes—a change of heart—which ultimately produces positive emotions and ways of thinking that transform how we behave and relate to others.

Through this journey the qualities of personal spiritual leadership begin to emerge. It starts by becoming dedicated to an inner life practice to develop a mindfulness that helps us to overcome unrealistic expectations based in emotional programs for happiness and cultural conditioning. This sets the stage for transformation of one's self-centered ego. Fueled by their inner life practice, spiritual leaders live life as a quest for unity and spiritual wellbeing. In doing so, they experience high levels of personal commitment and productivity in achieving their personal goals as well as high levels of life satisfaction.

While remarkable, it is not necessary to have intense spiritual visions and experiences such as those reported by Lynne Sedgmore. No, Lynne's experience as a response to the human condition is available to everyone. All the world's spiritual and religious traditions offer this promise. One way to experience a spiritual awakening can be the "burning bush" variety like Lynne, which is experienced as a sudden and spectacular upheaval or "God-consciousness." More often though, people have what William James (1985), in the *Varieties of Religious Experience*, calls the "educational variety," whereby their spiritual awareness develops slowly over a period of time.

As the saying goes, "None of us leave this world alive." We all face the ultimate conversion experience. While most people face the personal trials that create the potential for a spiritual awakening much later in life than Lynne, we all ultimately face it. Many choose not to embark on the spiritual journey to examine their emotional programs for happiness and cultural conditioning and the role these play in creating suffering through anger, resentment, worry, and fear. Those that do embark discover that what happens in life actually does not matter; it's all about the journey.

Practical Tools

For those interested in implementing spiritual leadership to maximize the triple bottom line, the major tools introduced in this chapter include:

1. *Personal leadership*—The self-confident ability to crystallize your thinking, establish an exact direction for your life, commit yourself to moving in that direction, and then take determined action to acquire, accomplish, or become whatever you identify as your ultimate goal in life.

2. *The personal spiritual leadership model*—Provides a roadmap for strong personal leadership based on a vision of service to others through altruistic love to maximize personal commitment and productivity, psychological wellbeing, and life satisfaction.

3. *Spiritual journey*—The process of seeking our true inner self through self-transcendence—the transformation from ego-centered to other-centered consciousness, while striving to attain and maintain a state of being or consciousness moment-to-moment.

4. *Mindfulness*—Provides the foundation for inner life, the spiritual journey, and maintaining a state of being or consciousness from moment-to-moment.

3

Developing Organizational Spiritual Leadership

From 1989 until taking over CEL as CEO in 2004, Lynne continued to develop her organizational spiritual leadership through various positions of increasing responsibility in the learning and skills sector. Throughout this period her guiding vision was to co-create healthy, loving, high performance organizations that nourish and develop the spirit and potential of both staff and learners.

Lynne Sedgmore's Organizational Spiritual Leadership

The model of organizational spiritual leadership mirrors that of the personal spiritual leadership model (see Figure 3.1). Personal spiritual leadership is practiced and developed though leadership roles, whether they are in family, community, spiritual/religious, non-profit, or for-profit organizations. Organizational spiritual leadership involves motivating and inspiring workers through a vision of love and service to key stakeholders. It also builds vision and value congruence across individual, team, and organiza-

Spiritual Leadership in Action, pages 33–42
Copyright © 2013 by Information Age Publishing

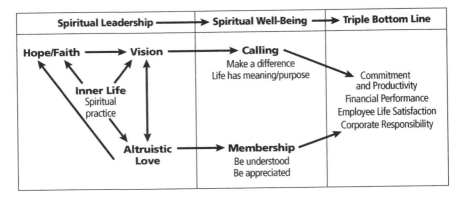

Figure 3.1   Model of organizational spiritual leadership.

tion levels to foster higher levels of employee wellbeing, sustainability, and financial performance.

Organizational spiritual leadership requires:

1. *An organizational vision* that pictures a journey through which leaders and followers experience a sense of calling so their lives have purpose and meaning and make a difference.
2. *An organizational culture* based on the values of altruistic love so that leaders and followers have a sense of membership and belonging, feel understood and appreciated, and have genuine care, concern, and appreciation for both self and others.

The source of organizational spiritual leadership is a context that supports employees' inner life, which provides the foundation for organizational spiritual leadership through hope/faith in a vision of service of key stakeholders through altruistic love. Organizational spiritual leadership then taps into spiritual wellbeing through calling and membership, which then fosters higher levels of organizational commitment and productivity, employee life satisfaction, financial performance, and corporate responsibility—the triple bottom line. A positive triple bottom line reflects an increase in the organization's value, including its human and societal capital as well as its profitability and economic growth.

Head of Croydon Business School (CBS)

As the head of the Croydon Business School (CBS) from 1989 through to 1994, Lynne managed a curriculum portfolio of over 30 higher education programs, 50 full-time staff, and more than 50 part-time staff. During her tenure she worked to improve the school's strategic vision and strategy, quality, curriculum, staff development, and business systems. It was in this role that Lynne began to develop organizational spiritual leadership through her attempt to integrate her spiritual values and her professional life. She discovered a new sense of work as her calling or true vocation. In doing so she became a Benedictine Oblate, studied the rule of Benedict, and used it as a model for developing her organizational spiritual leadership. The Benedictine vows are *conversatio* (continual learning and transformation), *simplicity*, and *chastity*. The role of the Abbot of the monastery is to lead by spiritual values, consensus, and a clear commitment to God through prayer, labor, and love.

It was clear that in a business school environment the words "God" or "spirituality" would not be acceptable; there was even discussion during the school's values consultation as to whether the word "fun" was acceptable. During this period, Lynne was in the vanguard of UK academic business schools using values as a mainstay and critical element of their business and operational plan. One of her major initiatives was to introduce a values clarification process based on the "7 S model" of *shared values, staff, structures, systems, services, standards,* and *stakeholders*. It was during this process that the staff adapted the model to add students at the center as well as shared values.

Lynne also experimented with collective and collaborative inquiry days, away days, and new processes that encouraged staff to work more horizontally and share professional expertise. As a result of these activities, a new sense of community arose among the staff, who were used to working in silos and competing for scarce resources with other departments. She also became more skilled in organizing collective days that worked effectively in fostering teamwork, clarity of purpose, and ensuring a new sense of belonging. These experimental activities were often challenged and questioned by the senior managers of the college, resulting in conflicts at times. Initially Lynne was thrown off balance and hurt by this negative feedback, but eventually she learned how to manage upwards to protect the good work her staff was involved in and to draw on the support of those who supported what she was doing.

A key lesson in all of this was the importance of delivering results and exceeding performance goals as the best protection against attack and envy. Subsequently, her senior team introduced a major culture change program that led to a 30% increase in fee income in addition to improved teamwork and quality control. In addition, the improved performance of CBS was verified from a range of external sources. These include:

- CBS being awarded a grade one (the highest level), which denotes outstanding or excellent, in the Office for Standards in Education (OFSTED) inspection in 1993. OFSTED is the national government inspection agency that reviews the quality of curriculum and standards every four years of all schools and colleges in England.
- being one of the first business schools to be accredited as a Management Charter Initiative Centre (MCI) and introducing innovative management NVQs, (National Vocational Qualifications).
- the CBS business plan being praised by several vocational higher education institutions who wrote to Lynne and asked if they could use its innovative structure and content for their own planning purposes

Evidence of the strong sense of vision and a caring culture that CBS formed over the next four years emerged when college reorganization took place in 1994. All but six of the CBS staff signed a petition saying that they did not want to be separated into two faculties under the new restructure proposal because they loved working in CBS and felt such a sense of empowerment, achievement, and pride in their performance

As the performance and quality of the school improved significantly, Lynne continued to encounter a number of professional relationship problems, conflicts, and misunderstandings that needed to be worked through. At the time she had little experience dealing with these kinds of issues. Consequently, she made several mistakes in terms of staff appointments and interventions. These experiences reinforced the critical importance of how she had to continue her own personal spiritual journey so as not to be seriously derailed and prevented from living what she felt was her true leadership path. This led her to begin a daily spiritual practice of meditation and prayer. She began going to a monastery on a regular basis to be in worship and silence. She also undertook bodywork with a holistic therapist on a weekly basis and went on retreats as often as she could amidst her busy schedule.

Lynne attended leadership development programs that focused on the importance of leadership qualities such as character as well as the more technical skills of leadership. She discovered leadership writers who wrote about the spirit and joined a group committed to learning how to live transformational leadership. She also undertook a post graduate MSc in Change Agent Skills and Strategies in a highly experiential program that enabled her to link her personal and professional learning on change and leadership in a more integrated manner. It was during this period that she learned about the Enneagram, a personality tool for understanding how differently people view the world and how they respond differently in the same situations.

Lynne's sense of organizational spiritual leadership was emerging. As she faced many professional challenges she found that her inner life spiritual practice was an important resource and source of nourishment. However, she was still aware of a disconcerting level of separation in aspects of her personal life and professional work. At times she could lead from love and a deep sense of connection to her higher purpose; but there were times when her personality took over, and she experienced doubt and fear and uncertainty.

Vice Principal Academic Croydon College

Lynne was promoted and served as vice principal higher education and then as vice principal academic at Croydon College from 1994 to 1998. In these roles she managed the operational and developmental aspects of the vocational and higher education curriculum, including equal opportunity programs. She also had the responsibility for all academic schools, which included 400 staff, 14,000 students, and revenue of over £20 million.

External accolades included:

- The highly prestigious Sussex University becoming a strategic partner for higher education (HE) programs, followed by the successful accreditation through Sussex of eleven degree and master's programs;
- The establishment of a new University Centre for all higher level programs, which was very uncommon at this time and led to increased enrolments and additional funding from the national HE funding body;
- The development of an innovative modular framework for all further educations programs, which was acclaimed by national sector agencies and used as a regional curriculum pilot; and
- The establishment of one of the first in-house, and highly success-ful, management development programs for college managers.

During this period Lynne developed and executed a challenging and successful higher education strategy and corporate academic plan for the entire college. As a member of the corporate senior management team, she led a college-wide visioning and values clarification process. It was during this period that she became affectionately known as "the values lady" and the "conscience of the college," although some staff were deeply resistant, suspicious, and even antagonistic to what she was doing.

Lynne became more skilled in exercising organizational spiritual leadership as she continually found herself forming new teams and co-creating a strong sense of membership and a spirited, creative community that placed the students at the heart of all they did. Her approach included team building, clear targets and the necessary support for achieving them, authentic dialogue and inquiry for creativity and problem solving, and a rigorous and generous program of staff development for both their personal growth and professional development. All of this was framed within a culture steeped in altruistic corporate values that were developed over several months in an open and transparent manner.

As Lynne was acquiring a reputation for fostering high performing teams and generating significant surplus income, she remarried and experienced an increased sense of integration of her inner work and professional spheres. She trained as a spiritual director in the Christian tradition, as a spiritual healer with the National Federation of Spiritual Healers, took vows as an Oblate to Douai Abbey monastic community, and began a journey of exploring Catholicism and Christianity in more depth. There was also interfaith work at national and international levels that included participating in interfaith conferences, dialogues, and joint services across the major faith traditions. Time away on retreats continued to give her nourishment and inner peace. Both her personal and organizational spiritual leadership acquired new depth through this inner work and strong sense of love and service to her vocation and higher purpose. She could feel a more intuitive responsiveness and the ability to be more and more in the moment. She was feeling more confident in handling negative criticism from others concerning her spiritual approach to leadership. She also became more able to recognize and contain her own negative personality traits and was gaining better insight into how she was both effective and flawed as a leader.

Principal and Chief Executive Guildford College

At age 42, Lynne was appointed the principal (president/CEO) of Guildford College and served for six years, from 1998 to 2004. As the new CEO, she inherited a budget of £15 million, 660 staff, and over 19,000 students. At that time student success was 48%, staff morale was low, and there was a deficit of £3m. With her senior team she improved communication and introduced major culture change, performance management, and e-learning throughout the college (Report from the Inspectorate, 2000). In 2001 the college was named as one of the UK's top 100 visionary organizations (Too Good for Max Clifford, 2001) and was presented the "Good Corporation" award for the college achieving a high level of corporate social responsibility (Best Practice: Guilford College, 2001). This was her first foray into the notion of the triple bottom line. The college also achieved the Business Excellence, Bronze Award for the high quality of its curriculum and services.

In 2003 Lynne led a successful merger with a smaller land based/agricultural college and was well established as a leader in the FE sector's *Success for All* initiative targeted at developing a framework for quality and success for all learners (A Sensible Way Forward, 2003). This involved the addition of a 400 acre site, 200 staff, 5,000 students, and new curriculum areas such as animal care. Her senior management team monitored all aspects of the merger and ensured an effective outcome based on respecting the culture of the smaller merging college while encouraging open dialogue and a climate of honoring the best from both very different cultures.

When Lynne left in 2004, the college budget was £28 million with 890 staff and 24,000 students. Student success was 84%, staff morale had significantly increased, and there was a £400k surplus. The college improved overall efficiency by 10%, improved student achievement by 26%, and increased student retention to 86%, while significantly increasing Guildford's national and local reputation. Moreover, a report by the national agency Investors In People (IPP) praised the college's strong and effective leadership, the raising of standards, strong support of students, the professional development of staff, and the wide range of effective partnerships. In recognition of these achievements Queen Elizabeth awarded Lynne the Commander of the British Empire (CBE), which is the second highest British honor, next only to Damehood.

During this period Lynne became the subject of a doctoral thesis, *Leaders and Spirituality—A Case Study* (Joseph, 2002). This thesis explored in depth and from different perspectives Lynne as a leader who is spiritually motivated and sought to apply workplace spirituality within her organization. The primary research was in two associated parts: a phenomenological description and analysis of Lynne as the newly appointed principal and chief executive of Guildford College; then, a longitudinal case study (18 months) covering a period of profound change within the college that incorporated data from interviews with six staff members. The thesis compares Lynne's organizational spiritual leadership style and interpersonal approach as espoused by her and as experienced by her staff and leadership team. Underlying processes were inferred that considered the impact of Lynne as a leader and the possible links among leadership, power, and spiritual influence.

The findings indicate that (1) a leader's spiritual motivation, while not likely to be perceptible to most observers, can have a significant and positive impact on an organization and, more specifically, on individuals within it; (2) proximity to the leader is highly significant; (3) explicit articulation of spiritual motivation can be expected to provoke significant reaction, which may sometimes be negative; and (4) leaders who are strongly motivated by spiritual beliefs seem likely to draw strength from beyond themselves. Finally, the impact of spiritual motivation as an additional dimension of competent leadership is potentially of profound significance to the individual leader, having consequences in the outer world dependent upon personal manifestation.

Relative to Lynne and her organizational spiritual leadership, the study concluded that:

- Lynne headed a high impact and far reaching change program and appeared proficient, competent, and effective in her role. Her starting point was inauspicious, with a legacy of unhelpful management practices in the past, though this could be seen as helpful to her by comparison, as long as her approach is viewed as successful. Against considerable inertia, and in difficult external circumstances, there were clear indications of progress and success.
- Her espoused style and approach in her role as principal and chief executive correlated closely with what is experienced by others in their relationships with Lynne. The data indicated that she was consistent over time and strongly asserted a values based approach.
- Proximity to and regular contact with Lynne was highly correlated with her degree of impact and influence. This proximity had a direct effect in terms of speed and effectiveness when establishing trust, gaining commitment, engendering loyalty, and motivating individuals.
- She developed a committed, cohesive and effective executive management team who were very loyal to her. They were well motivated, accepted significant responsibilities, and took on high workloads, sometimes at considerable personal cost. They appeared inclined to develop and hold common positions on some topics (as might be expected) that were significantly influenced by her, although there were indications that this team may have some blind spots. The study did not seek to understand the impact of this, and there was limited data from which to draw inferences.
- Lynne was perceived as working at a fast rate, being eager to take on all necessary projects and tasks and achieve objectives in as short a time as possible. She drove herself and others hard in the process, some said to an unreasonable degree.

- She was spiritually aware and motivated and guided in all that she did in the light of this awareness. Her past spiritual experiences had enlightened, reinforced, and underscored her awareness and her sense that she is "in service" to God and to others.
- She had a strong sense of mission about her job: a belief that she was "meant" to be in this role in this specific organization. She was strongly convinced of the value of integrating spirituality into the workplace and would wish it to be a place where "people can bring all of themselves here into the organization." She attempted to be aware of spirituality in small things and act appropriately on this awareness: "that's what transforms an organization, the small little encounters that touch the soul or heart or whichever bit of them that needed to be touched."
- The way Lynne operated within her organization and the results achieved can be considered an outstanding example of organizational spiritual leadership in action in the workplace.

Most staff were unaware of Lynne's spiritual beliefs, with the exception of those in close proximity to her, who were very aware, as she was very overt in discussing her particular beliefs and how they influence her.

Spirituality is a concept that was not usually considered by the majority of the research participants (and possibly a majority of all staff), either in the abstract or in relation to their own self-awareness or experience; most did not speak of it from personal experiential reflection. When faced with discussing it, there was, in almost all cases, a high degree of discomfort. When asked, most people proposed definitions related to their own strongly held principles and values; they also associated it with religion.

Joseph concluded that competent leaders exert significant influence within their organizations and particularly on those who work in close proximity to them. Where leaders are spiritually motivated, this does have an impact, but is generally unlikely to be attributed to spiritual causes by others. Making spirituality explicit as a belief and source of motivation is likely to provoke significant reaction that may not always be positive, though for some it will not only be positive but can have a profound personal impact, prompting introspection that may lead to further personal or spiritual development. The most significant difference for spiritually motivated leaders themselves is likely to be in their sense of personal mission and purpose within a wider, transcendent context—potentially sustaining or enhancing inspiration, motivation, persistence, and justification for commitment of energy and effort.

Conclusion

Overall, the period from 1989 to 2004 in Lynne's career demonstrates that one can develop *leading* skills through personal spiritual leadership. By cultivating a strong inner life practice, she acquired hope/faith in a transcendent vision of love and service to students, staff, and key stakeholders in the FE sector. This produced a sense of spiritual wellbeing through calling and membership that, ultimately, fueled higher levels of personal commitment, productivity, and personal wellbeing. In practicing personal spiritual leadership through encounters in various organizational roles with increasing responsibility, Lynne was able to develop organizational spiritual *leadership* skills that focused on the collective social influence process to engage everyone and enable groups of people to work together in meaningful ways. In doing so she engaged the organization and supported a context for workplace spirituality that nurtured and supported the inner life of workers and hope/faith in an organizational vision of service to key stakeholders based on the cultural values of altruistic love.

Practical Tools

For those interested in implementing spiritual leadership to maximize the triple bottom line, the major tools introduced in this chapter include:

1. *Leading versus leadership*—Provides an important distinction between *leading*, which focuses on leader development through the *personal* spiritual leadership model to achieve important personal outcomes, and *leadership*, where the focus is on the collective social influence process through the *organizational* spiritual leadership model to engage everyone and enable groups of people to work together in meaningful ways.

2. *Organizational spiritual leadership model*—Focuses on leadership development to build the capacity for better individual and collective adaptability and performance. Provides a roadmap for organizational spiritual leadership based on a vision of service to key stakeholders through altruistic love.

4

CEL

Set Up, Disarray, and a New Beginning

Lynne's previous job experiences allowed her to hone both her personal and organizational spiritual leadership. Her next assignment would put both to the test. For over four years Lynne Sedgmore led the national Centre for Excellence in Leadership (CEL) for the learning and skills sector, delivering a wide range of leadership and management services to over 40,000 participants with an annual budget for 2005/2006 of £2 million, which was renegotiated to over £16 million for 2006/2007.

Phase One—Oct 2003 to April 2004: Set Up and Disarray

CEL was formed initially through a national bidding process in 2003 that was commissioned by the then Department for Education and Skills (DFES). Bids were solicited for the creation of this organization (worth £14 million over three years) to set up a new national leadership center for further education (FE). The purpose of this new organization was to raise the bar of leadership for principals of the 300 FE colleges, CEOs of 2,000 training

Spiritual Leadership in Action, pages 43–54
Copyright © 2013 by Information Age Publishing
43

agencies, plus their senior staff and middle managers. This was to be a significant intervention in bringing the English national learning and skills sector up to world class standards. CEL was intended to be experimental in creating a more entrepreneurial form of organization. The business model was that CEL was to be a company, funded by contract, limited by shares, with an independent board, and relatively autonomous from government. It was launched officially on October 8, 2003 by Margaret Hodge—the then Education Minister—and Anita Roddick, CEO of the Body Shop. The winning team was a partnership of:

- LSDA—Learning and Skills Development Agency, an FE sector national government funded agency responsible for FE curriculum and practitioner support and development. It ceased to exist when it became the Quality Improvement Agency (QIA) in 2006. They were the lead agency.
- LUMS—Lancaster University Business School, renowned for its work in leadership development, leadership evaluation, and as a top-ranked research university.
- Ashridge Business School, a prestigious independent business school, highly ranked in Europe and a major player in leadership development in the corporate world. Ashridge's campus has stunningly beautiful surroundings, and it had a strong international reputation.

This three-way partnership was considered a massive coup in that such prestigious organizations would be supporting and developing the learning and skills sector, although there was some resentment in FE colleges that higher education (HE) organizations were being brought in to sort the sector out. There is a long running issue in the UK that FE is considered lesser than HE.

CEL was led initially by an interim CEO from LSDA and a senior team made up from the three partners. The board members were from two of the partner organizations and one independent member. CEL was funded with a budget of £14m over three years and given annual targets of 500 participants per annum and customer satisfaction of 75%. Its main target was to achieve 1,500 participants by March 2006, on specified annual budgets of £6.2m in year one, £5.8m in year two, and £2m in year three. CEL was also to be financially self-sufficient by March 2006, a target that was overly ambitious and eventually precipitated CEL's downfall.

The partners had never worked together, although between them they had a massive pool of expertise and resources. While in theory all this was wonderful, there were a number of issues that created a range of difficulties from the beginning.

- The LUMS research team introduced a research program more closely aligned to their own research interests and needs rather than ones desired by or relevant to the sector customers. This meant that trust and rapport on research was never established, and, since £3 million of the £14 million budget was allocated to research, this became a significant resource matter and led to a bitter dispute. Over three years any interventions to make the research program more applied and accepted by the FE sector were resisted by the research team.
- While some of the programs and staff of Ashridge and LUMS were effective, there were major issues of relevance, and it became apparent that the FE colleges wanted leadership interventions based more on direct knowledge and understanding of FE.
- The LUMS and Ashridge overhead charge was 78%. While this is not an unusual figure and was agreed upon in the contract, it meant that there were no resources left to provide any assets to CEL. By April 2004, the end of the first financial year, £6.2 million had been spent by the partner organizations, and CEL did not have a single asset, not even a computer. The second year budget of £5.8 million was planned, before Lynne's appointment, in a similar vein.
- CEL was meant to be financially self sufficient by March 2006. It was clear that this was impossible with the approach at hand and that the partners had no workable plan to make CEL a viable entity. The budget left for the third year was £2 million. This was a daunting challenge for the new CEO and one that had to be tackled with extreme urgency.
- The partners did not always assign their best staff, resources, and researchers to the CEL "project."
- Each of the three partners had very different leadership pedagogies that could not be reconciled in a complementary manner, despite many attempts to do so.
- The cultures of the three partners were very different and frequently clashed. It was hard for partner staff to give allegiance to CEL, as their own organizations were safer and more prestigious, although a group of staff from LSDA and a range of individuals from LUMS and Ashridge gradually moved their loyalties and employment contracts to CEL on a voluntary basis.

The newly formed CEL organization was committed to carrying out innovative research on leadership across the learning and skills sector as well as commissioning a number of academic and practitioner research projects through a national bidding process. However, the three partners had never worked together, everyone was on assignment, no one was employed directly by CEL, and the interim CEO had never been in a CEO role before. Because of all this, it soon became clear that the CEO was having difficulty pulling the new senior team together. In addition, all the incentives, financial and otherwise, were geared to encouraging loyalty and commitment to the partners rather than to CEL. All the first year's funding was paid to partners in development costs with only 90 participants going through programs from October to April. The new CEL project was potentially high risk, so staff remained committed to the perks and positions within their host institutions.

There were also serious conflicts between the partners on leadership pedagogy, nature of programs, the nature of research, commitment to the sector, and who should/could dominate and be the lead partner. The interim CEO was not able to surface any of these tensions. The team was dysfunctional and worked primarily based on partner interests. Partners frequently used their own organizational names when working with participants rather than the CEL name and brand. CEL program participants consistently reported that they experienced three separate organizations, not one.

Another complication was that the FE colleges felt resentful that two HE organizations had been brought in to "sort out" their leadership when there was a strong desire and belief that the sector could do this for themselves. The sector sensed that the CEL partners were not highly committed and as a result had very low trust and belief that CEL could be effective.

As a Ministerial project overtly supported at Ministerial and Secretary of State level, politically the CEL project had to be seen to be successful. However, the government's initial funding of £14m was public knowledge, so FE colleges were reluctant to pay fees to the CEL partner organizations and felt they were being "fleeced" by HE, a sector much wealthier and better funded than FE.

Achievements by April 2004 were dismal at best:

- 90 participants against a target of 500;
- All of the first year £6.2m budget spent;
- No assets owned by CEL;
- Most of the income had been paid to partners for development work;

- Management team created from senior staff of partners but not working collectively as a CEL team, so the main motivation for staff lay in creating value for partners;
- Major research program initiated and themes decided for £3m investment over three years with a focus on HE—not FE—interests;
- No additional income secured, thus 100% dependency on government funding; and
- Only five product lines in place.

Phase Two—April 2004 to March 2005—A New CEO

Lynne Sedgmore was appointed CEO in December 2003 and was scheduled to take over in April 2004. She was a popular choice, and most believed that she would "fix" the problems with CEL and do so in a manner and style congruent with FE sector values. As she had entered the sector in 1982, Lynne had wide and powerful networks. She was well known for publicly stating her love of the sector and her love of learning and of learners. She had a strong track record of success in leading colleges and a good reputation as a leadership thinker as well as a practicing leader. She believed that she had the trust and mandate of a majority of the sector.

The depth of the challenge, unknown to her at the time of her appointment, was quickly revealed. Initially she was devastated. It was only after much soul searching that she had decided to leave Guildford College, where she enjoyed significant success, recognized in her receiving the prestigious Commander of the Order of the British Empire (CBE) award from the Queen in 2004 for services to further education for the outstanding success and progress of Guildford College and its improvement in results. A major factor in her decision was her belief that the new leadership organization was in a good state and one she could significantly form and influence.

On examining the state of CEL, she soon realized that all was not as it seemed. Her initial analysis led Lynne to insist on an external audit two months before she formally took up her post. The result was a "red alert" highlighting major issues:

- financial stress,
- lack of CEL dedicated assets,
- low customer value for money across all services,
- conflict of interest at board level with board members also acting as contractors,
- no staff employed directly by CEL,

▪ contract overly favorable to partners, and
▪ serious tensions in working relations between CEL and the government department officials.

It was a crisis situation, but as proposed in the organizational spirituality model in Chapter 1, it also served by default, if not by design, as an impetus and driver for engendering a virtuous organization. It is at times like these that leaders gain the opportunity to create difference. Lynne seized the opportunity.

She had been thinking about and deliberating on this role for 10 months. While meditating at a retreat in Sri Lanka in the summer of 2003 and preparing to apply for the post of CEL CEO, she experienced a powerful and strong vision of CEL and her role as an organizational spiritual leader. She wrote a vision and set of aims for CEL that resonated within her own mind and soul. She had gone on another retreat in October 2003, before the interview, to ascertain if her desire for the job was based primarily in satisfying her own ego, or was the next "aligned" role for her and the next authentic step on her spiritual path. After much soul searching she felt strongly that this was a role she wanted for the right reasons and that it would enable her to continue her spiritual growth and development, as well as make a contribution to FE and her profession. In taking on this new role, Lynne drew especially on her inner life practices to develop a strong and clear vision of what CEL could be and the difference and impact it could make.

It was this spiritual "knowing" and certainty that enabled her to tackle and withstand the immense difficulties of the first 12 months at CEL. During the pre-employment period from January to April, she met with key players in CEL to ascertain the situation. She observed the following:

▪ a poor relationship between the ministry-level civil servants and the senior leadership team;
▪ spending of the total annual budget by partners and under-achievement of targets;
▪ significant tensions among partners, particularly on their pedagogies of management and leadership development; and
▪ insufficient development of new company structures, procedures, and processes to operate as an autonomous entity (e.g., inability to offer a CEL employment contract and pension scheme to the newly appointed CEO).

On the positive side Lynne discovered a highly motivated, experienced, and committed board and senior management team. What was lacking, in her assessment, was any corporate identity to the new organization. The operating teams were assigned only temporarily to CEL, so naturally their primary loyalties were to their home organizations. She also learned to her surprise that CEL was technically a subsidiary of the LSDA. This had not been made clear during the interview and appointment process. While respecting the technical and legal requirements, she moved her tiny team out to new office premises to signal CEL's desire for independence and autonomy, to the chagrin of some involved.

By the time Lynne Sedgmore took up her role as CEO of CEL in April 2004, she had undertaken significant exploration into the spiritual dimension of leadership. As part of her personal leadership journey she had tried to understand how her spirituality affected her practice of organizational spiritual leadership, its impact on the organization's culture, the development of followers into leaders, and the triple bottom line. The move to CEL was a period of transition in her new role as leader of a newly formed national leadership center and in her inner spiritual landscape and experiences.

Upon starting work, Lynne insisted on being the first employee directly employed by CEL even though her employment conditions were less favorable than being employed by one of the partners. She then attempted to develop an overarching corporate vision and set of cultural values. However, partner interests overrode continuously and resulted in too much game playing. After six months she decided to focus on areas of partner strength and to abandon an integrated approach, in the interest of achieving performance goals. CEL vision, values, and aims were established with minimum consultation due to the partner-based silo structure, partner mentality, and the need to achieve set targets in order not to be closed down in the following year. The vision, values, and aims were initially written by Lynne with input from the chair, senior team, and those few staff that shared her vision for CEL. She consistently made it clear this was not her preferred leadership style, but the circumstances demanded it since, without adequate program development and delivery of targets, CEL would not continue beyond March 2006.

She asked for trust on her current behaviors and promised to be held accountable in the next phase of CEL if her style did not change. The values were published as part of the *Leading the Way* document in November 2004 to:

> encourage a clear, confident, and consistent leadership voice that represents the FE sector and provide a respected and valued source of advice to

policy-makers and practitioners on key leadership issues and developmental requirements. (Centre for Excellence in Leadership, 2004, p. 3)

The staff understood her dilemma (some reluctantly) and were delighted when Lynne did indeed keep her word and introduced due process in 2005/2006, with an external facilitator to articulate shared values with all CEL staff invited to participate. The outcomes were articulated as follows:

CEL's vision:

- world-class educational leadership for every learner;
- outstanding leaders, providers, and partnerships; and
- inspired learning, learners, employers, and skills development.

CEL's mission:

- To improve the standard of leadership and the diversity and talent pool of leaders in the learning and skills sector (Quality, Equality, Quantity)

CEL's espoused organizational values:

- *Learner focused*—We empower and enable everyone we work with to achieve their full leadership potential.
- *Professional*—We are passionate, energetic, and dedicated professionals who deliver high standards and performance.
- *Reflective*—We are reflective practitioners continually improving our professionalism and seeking feedback.
- *Collaborative*—We are a partnership organization and believe in sharing our learning and expertise.
- *Creative*—We think outside the box and constantly seek innovative ways of seeing the world. We strive constantly to learn and improve and create an open and supportive culture.
- *Diverse*—We celebrate and respect our differences alongside ensuring inclusivity and equality of opportunity.

CEL's strategic aims:

- to improve the overall standard of leadership in the sector,
- to improve leadership of provider performance for learner and employer success,
- to improve the diversity profile of sector leaders,
- to improve the supply of leaders to ease the succession crisis, and

- to improve the quality and impact of research on leadership within the sector.

CEL's personal values:

- treating people with respect;
- professionalism, doing the best job for the sector;
- awareness, knowing what customers think and want;
- self-reflection about what is done well and what could be done better;
- honesty, integrity;
- principles around public service, value for money, good quality service;
- maintaining good relationships, within CEL and in the sector;
- openness;
- hard working; and
- equality, including social inclusion.

CEL's vision and values can be viewed as exemplars of the organizational spiritual leadership model. They served to create the context in which language, cultural, and intellectual difference could be transcended and practical actions enabled. They also provided the means by which each partner could make their own unique contribution within a framework that guided behaviors and responses to each other. Valuable time and energy had been put into revisiting, discussing, agreeing on, and affirming a shared vision, mission, aims, and values. Most individual staff related to and tried to live by the new values, and staff teams evolved and delivered what was needed because they now held and shared clear, strong values of professionalism and service to the leaders in the sector. They also cared passionately about their customers and learners and listened to them in order to provide the programs and services they most needed and wanted. Meanwhile, Lynne and her leadership team did everything they could to empower staff to do their best. From February 2005 onwards it became clear that a new, focused, and more unified CEL was forming, greatly supported by the dedicated work of CEL's board and its chairman, David Marshall.

A major achievement was to convince DFES to revise the whole funding base of CEL and to commit to a new budget of £15m for 2005–2007 (rather than the £2m already committed for 2005–2006) and to extend the financial self-sufficiency goal by 12 months to March 2007. A key factor in this decision was the fact that CEL had far exceeded their annual participant goal of training 500 participants by nearly 400%! There was also a significant increase in customer satisfaction and a commitment to generate 8,000 participants the following year for an investment of £7.5m. This was a big step in delivering value for the money invested.

CEL committed to raising the level of additional non-governmental funds and to tackle seriously the issue of becoming financially self-sufficient as soon as possible. From the beginning it had always been made clear that CEL had to ultimately be financially self-sufficient. The CEO and board had continually made projections and plans to ensure this. A major impediment to achieving financial self-sufficiency was the reluctance of the sector organizations to pay sufficient fees for the services offered. For example, the Aspiring Principal's Senior Management Program cost £6,000. In other sectors and business schools a comparative program cost from £12,000 to £24,000. Despite this knowledge, FE colleges refused to pay more than £6k. Indeed, colleges continued to insist that £6k was exorbitant despite many discussions with the advisory group and key stakeholders. Although this was understandable since the FE colleges in general felt under-funded and had not yet developed a culture of investing significant sums in the development of its senior managers, it still was a major roadblock to CEL's goal of self-sufficiency. The senior team had managed to get CEL formally off the red alert audit status to green status in a period of 12 months. This took a tremendous amount of hard work and dedication by many staff, but it was achieved. This meant that Ministers and senior civil servants could now give overt support to CEL without fear of embarrassment.

CEL received public support and endorsement from the new Secretary of State for Education, Alan Johnson, and the new Minister for Higher and Further Education, Bill Rammell, was a frequent speaker at CEL events and encouraged the entrepreneurial activity of CEL. Indeed the then Prime Minister, Tony Blair, wrote a complimentary foreword for the CEL 2006/2007 annual review.

CEL began to organize high profile conferences and events that were creative, imaginative, and highly valued as evidenced by good attendance and positive feedback from customers and stakeholders. A hallmark of CEL became the unusual venues it used across the country to hold its events, a key element of the magic of CEL and one of its differences from other national organizations. Examples included: the rooftop gardens in Kensington, which had live flamingos walking in its grounds and beautiful gardens across the rooftops of London; the Globe Shakespeare Theatre; the famous oval cricket grounds; the Arsenal football Emirates stadium; beautiful country manor houses; a haunted hotel; the Tower of London; and a Thames river cruise boat with the Tower of London Bridge opening especially for guests.

Conclusion

CEL's beginning was tumultuous at best and seemed doomed to fail from the start. No initial attempt was made to create a unified vision and organizational culture for CEL by its partner organizations. High administrative overheads meant that resources were funneled to partners' institutions rather than for fueling a new, innovative, financially self-sufficient public sector organization. Projects that were funded were well aligned with the partners' expertise and interests, but possibly less so with the expressed needs of the FE sector that CEL was intending to serve.

The partners rarely assigned their best staff or researchers to developmental projects. Differences in culture, leadership pedagogy, and the inevitable power struggles made it hard for staff, who still reported to their respective partners, to become loyal and committed to CEL. Plus the FE colleges in general were hesitant to pay sufficiently for CEL's programs. Not surprisingly, CEL performed poorly during this initial period, with program participation way below target and no additional participants or revenue from non-governmental agencies.

Upon her appointment as CEO in December 2003, Lynne Sedgmore was not aware of these problems or the fact that CEL was not a fully autonomous agency. However, the initial analysis and external audit she commissioned before she started in April 2004 made clear the depth and seriousness of the challenges she faced. Lynne realized that if CEL was to have a new beginning, she would need to draw heavily on her inner life and personal spiritual leadership to weather the many storms that she would face. She also drew heavily from past experience and her commitment to organizational spiritual leadership as she worked with the partners and staff in (1) developing CEL's vision, cultural values, and strategic aims; (2) moving CEL from red alert to green audit status; (3) exceeding training goals; (4) revising CEL's funding base; and (5) extending the financial self-sufficiency deadline.

Lynne's initial actions are an example of what any leader should do when key segments of the organization or the environment don't share the values of organizational spiritual leadership. Spiritual leadership does not mean that you do not use a command and control leadership style if that is what is necessary. It can be an appropriate response to a central dilemma that many leaders will face in trying to create a sphere of influence for implementing spiritual leadership when the leaders and their core units or groups of followers are embedded in a larger hostile organization or external environment.

Moreover, Lynne would soon discover that her past experience and approaches to leadership were of limited use for a new entrepreneurial venture like CEL. There would also be many more opportunities for spiritual growth and the need for further development and reinforcement of her inner life practice and the values, attitudes, and behavior necessary for her personal and organizational leadership. This would all be necessary if she were to effectively guide CEL from a troubled new startup to one that empowered all staff to maximize the triple bottom line through spiritual leadership.

Practical Tools

For those interested in implementing spiritual leadership to maximize the triple bottom line, the major tool introduced in this chapter is:

1. *Organizational vision and values based on spiritual leadership*—Provide the foundation for the organizational transformation necessary to love and serve key stakeholders and maximize the triple bottom line.

5

A Privileged Conversation

Democratizing Strategy Through Spiritual Leadership

Although intuitively Lynne knew that the approach she used in Guild-ford would not be best for CEL, she had no clear picture of what the alternative should be. There was also the added dimension of operating nationally in the political arenas of civil service and Ministerial requirements and sensitivities, a completely new experience for her. The transition from a CEO role leading a local community college to leading an entrepreneurial new venture at the national level was exciting and daunting.

She discovered that her primary preoccupation and leadership task was to understand the differences and difficulties her new role posed against her previous work. She began to experience this transition as much more demanding and painful than anything she could have prepared for. Lynne felt that she had lost all sense of comfort and confidence in her leadership intuition and ability, which left her in a deep place of unknowing, confusion, and deficiency. However, she found some solace in the fact that this was echoed in private conversation with other national leaders who had also struggled with the same transition.

Spiritual Leadership in Action, pages 55–70
Copyright © 2013 by Information Age Publishing

This signaled a new "dark night of the soul" for Lynne. Deep down she knew the only way to make the transition was in a way and style meaningful to her: one that served CEL and its staff and the sector leaders but that also served and honored her inner convictions. This honoring of her spirituality felt more central and delicate than it had ever been during her career, and she knew that, in addition to this major leadership and professional transition, her own inner life was changing, leaving her in turmoil and confusion.

Lynne had by then consistently worked with a spiritual director or counselor for some 20 years, but not with a personal executive coach. Now she knew that she needed help linked directly to her work in order to move through this major leadership challenge and felt an unprecedented need for the assistance of a professional coach to help her perform this new leadership role effectively. At the same time, she sensed her inner life needed special attention to help her focus on and expend more and more energy on ensuring the success of CEL.

Lynne chose an experienced executive coach, Dr. Simon Western, who could respond to and support her spiritual and inner life and also help integrate it with her professional development in organizational spiritual leadership. Dr. Western focuses on liberating individuals and teams to discover their "freedom to act." He helps leaders design organizational architectures that inspire creativity. Lynne had met Dr. Western in different capacities as a facilitator on CEL programs and on staff away days. She knew that he was an experienced executive coach and had a successful track record. Moreover, the CEL director of coaching recommended him highly and was sure he could maintain confidentiality while working in CEL. This was all Lynne needed to hear, and she soon booked an exploratory session with him.

Her exploratory conversation with Dr. Western went well. They talked about professional issues, then gradually and naturally moved onto a sharing of their spiritual lives. The similarities were affirming, and yet there were also differences. She felt that here was someone that was aware of the complex issues facing CEL and who could greatly help her be a more effective leader as well as facilitate her spiritual growth. The core of her decision to use Simon lay in knowing that he was an effective, well qualified, and experienced coach with significant organizational experience; but most importantly, he had a conscious spiritual life of his own and an inner life he was prepared to share that was central to his own life and awareness. He made it clear though that he saw their coaching relationship primarily as a task-focused partnership to support the development of CEL as both an effective business and as a spiritual organization.

Under her leadership, CEL developed a range of coaching services for sector leaders, including a highly successful coaching leadership program based on solutions-focused coaching for individuals and teams. During this period, Dr. Western became director of a new coaching diploma within Lancaster University that trained professional coaches. CEL funded 12 Black-minority-ethnic (BME) coaches from the FE sector to train in this course so that more coaches from ethnic minorities could be developed to support BME leaders.

A Privileged Conversation

Dr. Western uses a framework with a focus on leadership development he calls "THINK coaching" that is psychodynamically informed (Western & Sedgmore, 2008). THINK coaching is designed to take leaders through a process that radically improves their capability to *think clearly* under pressure, to *think creatively*, and to *think collaboratively*. THINK coaching focuses on five basic components:

T   Thinking Space—the essence of coaching is to create a space to think

H   Hope—essential to create leverage for change

I   Imagination—accessing our intuitive and unconscious creativity

N   Network—taking the learning from the individual into his or her personal network is a vital stage for the coaching process

K   Knowledge Exchange—sharing knowledge in the network and finding leverage points to create sustainable change

THINK coaching is also based on the idea that creating a space to think is also about creating a potential space for the spirit/divine to become present and active within us. Thus both the coach and the coachee embrace and struggle with spiritual issues as a shared and active part of the work.

Lynne's coaching sessions lasted approximately two to two and a half hours with a short comfort break and a reflection break. She and Dr. Western generally met once a month, sometimes more often if they were working on an intense or urgent issue. The coaching intervention itself was aimed at providing Lynne with the safety to work on both personal and organizational spiritual issues as well as creating a space to engage with her spirituality as it arose. This meant holding the THINK space to allow the dilemmas and challenges facing Lynne to surface in spite of huge pressures to deliver and meet the seemingly impossible targets imposed by stakeholders.

Thinking Space. From Lynne's perspective the main impact of the coaching sessions was that it provided a safe space for her to push the boundaries of creating new organizational designs and processes for CEL. She found this experience to be enabling, liberating, and a further integration of her professional and spiritual life.

Hope. Lynne found the coaching space to be both sacred and professional. The whole experience was deeply liberating, and she began to sense a deeper and deeper integration and challenge as she weaved through and traveled both terrains. Her confidence in her ability to face the challenges before her returned as she gradually learned how to let go and began to accept the unknowable.

Imagination. In one of the early sessions, Dr. Western asked Lynne to draw a picture of how she wanted to be and how she was in her role as CEO of CEL. Lynne drew a confusing picture that echoed and paralleled the lack of structure in the organization she inherited.

Liberating the imagination to interpret and hypothesize about the picture, playing with ideas, free from the impositions of the need to finding solutions, Lynne began to realize the picture was one of the CEO as an atom sparking life to all around. Then came the realization that, while this had been Lynne's leadership style for many years in FE colleges, CEL was a more dispersed and virtual organization. Therefore, her earlier leadership approach wasn't going to work in the same way or be the template for success as it had been in the past.

Three powerful paradoxical themes emerged, which they then explored in depth:

1. Being both skinless (as in vulnerable) and ruthless (as in focused and determined, but not nasty);
2. Having control, yet influencing through empowerment; and
3. Experiencing and holding the paradox of unity and fragmentation rather than emphasizing one over the other.

Over several sessions Lynne was able to perceive and hold these and other paradoxes much more skillfully and with ease. The transition became less painful as she began to understand both the inner and external complexities and demands required of her in her new leadership role.

As Lynne's faith in her inner life as a source of personal spiritual leadership grew, she was able more and more to trust the new CEL staff. Together they could achieve and accomplish their shared goals, however impossible and difficult they seemed at times. She discovered also that even though her personality and ego would kick in at difficult times, she was more centered, trusting, and present in her work than before.

Network. At some stage of this work process, the imagination, thinking, and hope needed to be translated into the network of activity in the workplace. In reality this was an ongoing process as the above example showed, whereby Lynne's inner work was translated to outer work in her organization.

Together with Dr. Western, Lynne mapped the networks of activity of individuals, groups, departments, and stakeholders. These maps permitted power, relationships, communications, and creativity to be explored. This exercise allowed the "organization-in-the-mind" to be externalized, and once it was on paper it could be viewed and looked at from different angles.

They worked on this network map and returned many times to revise and to play with mapping the organizational structure until they discovered coherence to the organizational architecture that would work for CEL. Out of this network activity, Lynne was able to create a more liberating, less hierarchical structure and organizational form that was different in intention and shape than those she had co-created previously. The new organization was not hierarchical, but more an organic, learning organization (see Figure 5.1)—an organization steeped in a sense of service to the CEL learners, who are placed clearly at the center of the organization's purpose. Impact on the provider (customer) organizations is a key feature, as are stakeholders and CEL partners. In essence, this views the organization of CEL staff not as an end in itself but instead as a means to provide the best possible service, to fulfill relevant stakeholder expectations, and to respond to the major policy initiatives that drove CEL's funding, but that CEL was also keen to shape and influence. The diagram was also intended to engender a sense of interconnectedness in a circular rather than a linear format.

As the sessions progressed, her spirit lifted, and Lynne could feel her energy increase. She also became more confident in naming and challenging the competition and fragmentation within CEL by encouraging open debate on living CEL's espoused values. As this process unfolded, she discovered that some of her old defenses were resurfacing: in particular her irritation and anger at staff who were underperforming or creating blockages within the organization. With this realization, she found her serenity and calm got lost with particular staff in far less extreme circumstances than previously.

Lynne has always had a fiery nature and was quick to speak her mind and tell people when she thought they were neglecting their duties. On one occasion she did verbally "tell off" four administrators during a conference when no one was available in the room to support a speaker, and she

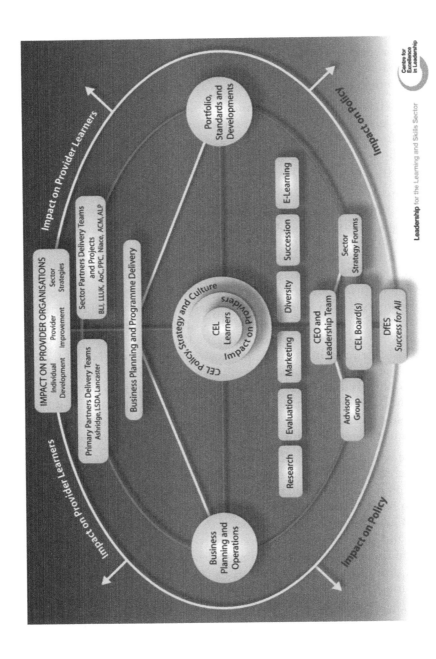

Figure 5.1 CEL organizational and functional structure.

found them outside "chatting" (as she perceived it). In a coaching session, Dr. Western proposed to Lynne that she was seen by these administrators, and through the spreading of the story, to have abused her power as CEO and to have acted inappropriately. Through the coaching, Lynne was able to see that she was not acting in altruistic love in verbally shouting at staff, however inappropriate their behavior at the time, and that she had not bothered to follow up on the effects of her actions, nor had she listened to their side of the story.

Lynne then went deeper, with Dr. Western's support, into her ego defenses of "being right" and explored the role of a CEO in a learning organization. She could see clearly that the onus was on her to make an amend. After meditation and soul searching, she decided that she needed to make a public acknowledgment of what she had done and offer an apology, hopefully in a manner that also provided an opportunity for her to be more transparent and to open a two-way dialogue.

She did this during her introduction at the next staff away day. This was not easy for Lynne to do; she felt emotional and vulnerable as she spoke the words of apology. She felt she had let herself and her staff down and behaved in a manner that was neither spiritual nor professional. As she spoke the words of regret and apology, she felt as if a weight was lifting off her. Her words were met with silence. She was tearful, but it seemed to her at the time the staff believed she was sincere. During the break individual staff approached her and said how much they welcomed her words since it had been an issue where they had felt "let down." Her actions had been incongruent with the values of CEL and her own espoused leadership style. Some of those concerned shared how frightened that felt as they feared she might change and take away what they valued, or that CEL's values were not real.

This incident brought home to Lynne the importance of how a leader's actions impact on a daily basis upon the staff experience of membership and community. It also punctuated how fragile trust and the collective sense of wellbeing could be at times. After this incident, Lynne sought feedback from staff to assist her in not repeating such behavior and asked for their feedback if it seemed to be happening again. She also asked that they all reflect on their part in any situation of conflict or difference within CEL so that they take responsibility as a community and co-create a space in which they could manage conflict effectively.

Knowledge Exchange. The knowledge exchange part of the framework is how the coachee finds the resources and knowledge within the system and shares her discoveries and ideas. Knowledge exchange is about how to make the next step to implement ideas. It works on the assumption that this is not top-down knowledge sharing, but a real exchange where leverage points in the system have to have the information to enable success to flourish.

Lynne's personal work focused on her own concept of spiritual leadership, in other words, how she loved and served others in her role as CEO and dealt with personal challenges. The systemic work focused on her organizational spiritual leadership with an emphasis on strategic thinking in working on the organizational architecture and thinking holistically and systemically.

For example, as mentioned earlier, the initial conduct of the senior management team, made up of individuals from across the network of partner institutions, was problematic and dysfunctional. They were on assignment from their home organizations and not necessarily the best people for reinforcing and accomplishing CEL's vision, values, and aims. The development of the partnership had involved significant differences in style, values, reasons for engagement, and leadership pedagogy. No real team building had been undertaken, and tensions were high. Lynne and her team soon realized that to focus on the differences and tensions, or worse, on the individuals involved, would just add to an already dysfunctional situation.

It was through systemic thinking and imagination that they were able to look through a different lens and ask the unthinkable: why do we need a senior management team in this form? What would CEL look like without one? This question and the insights gleaned from it led to the successful initiative that saw a new CEL board and senior team appointed. After receiving an additional two years of significant public funding, the decision was made to reorganize CEL into a charitable trust and to reconstitute the board, with a new model of transparency. CEL would move away from the three year contract with the partners and become a completely independent organization that could contract with any party; it would no longer be a formal subsidiary of the Learning Skills and Development Agency (LSDA). Eight new board members were appointed after a national search process. The board now included highly respected and influential people from a range of sectors, including local authorities, health, further education, and the charity sector. It was the most diverse board in terms of equality and diversity of any FE national agency.

In all, five new executive and six non-executive members were appointed. The new senior management team comprised one deputy CEO and seven directors:

- Ivor Jones—Deputy CEO
- Helen Pettifor—Director of Programs and Services

- Yvette Adams—Director of Diversity, Culture, and Organizational Development
- Steve Hutchinson—Director of Finance
- Diana Watson—Director of Marketing
- Caroline Mager—Director of Policy
- Jo Clough—International Director
- Professor David Collinson—Director of Research

Each brought his or her own specific talents and professional expertise and had significant previous experience of successfully working at senior corporate levels. They valued and respected each other and were open to working collaboratively, transparently, and sharing leadership power. Most importantly they were keen to work on themselves and had a genuine desire to be reflective practitioners. Although their leadership styles were very different, they shared similar core values, a genuine sense of service to others, plus a strong commitment to students and the FE sector. Yet the leadership team was not without challenges and difficulties as real issues, tensions, and conflicts had to be aired and worked through in order for the new team to perform effectively.

The governance of CEL was a key factor in CEL's success, and staff often expressed a view that the CEL board was different than any other board they had ever experienced. The chair and the eight board members worked as a genuine team and welcomed and actively sought input for decision making from all levels of CEL. In particular, David Marshall as chair, Nick Acacrombie as vice chair and Ann Limb—a key board member—strongly supported Lynne as CEO and her attempt to implement organizational spirituality and maximize the triple bottom line through spiritual leadership. Ann, in particular, was overt in her support of Lynne's work on spirituality in CEL and was also a key champion of this field nationally within the FE sector.

In sum, during the early coaching sessions Lynne spent time with Dr. Western drawing network maps of the system as a whole and the relationships within it and also personal maps of how she saw herself in the organization. They worked hard and fast, bouncing ideas around and discussing how her leadership style and assumptions needed to adapt to lead this new organizational structure. She realized that to lead a startup organization like CEL was a new challenge that required enabling leadership to be distributed throughout the organization.

Lynne also worked also on personal issues, including how she managed her leadership role and her relationships with her fellow workers. In parallel she and Dr. Western worked on the strategic and structural issues of the system. They also agreed that the leadership task was to create the structures and culture to allow CEL as an organization to develop itself through entrepreneurial activity and to deliver at local levels while having a collective identity, common processes, and branding. After coming up with a picture that represented the organizational architecture that could deliver some of the desired structural changes, it was time to implement them.

Democratizing Strategy Through Spiritual Leadership

With her coach's help, Lynne introduced a series of strategy forums with the aim of democratizing strategy within CEL so that it involved staff at every level and was not solely the domain of the board and top leaders. In doing so, Lynne delivered on her earlier promise that full staff engagement is her true leadership style and desire. Over the next two years, she drew upon her maturing personal and organizational spiritual leadership and introduced a new phase in which CEL staff were invited formally to reinforce and co-create the vision and values of the organization they wanted CEL to be. This process resulted in staff responding with renewed responsibility, accountability, and trust. A key aspect of this phase was the creation of strategic consultation and decision forums, which had two goals:

1. to democratize strategy by creating an inclusive strategic process that would also create opportunities for more distributed leadership; and
2. to create an organizational forum that allowed creativity, communication, and emergent ideas to flow from all parts of the organization.

The strategic forums were structured and facilitated to resist the rush to premature closure. This freed the participants from the pressure of coming up with action plans, while at the same time encouraging "truthful engagement" and avoiding negative thinking. The forum was designed to foster these desired outcomes by providing:

1. space to (non) think;
2. space to connect, communicate, and network;
3. space to be creative; and
4. activities that "unbalanced" and deconstructed normative responses.

The major task of the forums was to create a new space from which open communication and new thinking could occur and to offer ideas and interventions that would contribute to the emerging strategy. The aim of these interventions was to introduce into CEL a form and structure that acted as both a signifier and a conduit of change. It simultaneously provided physical spaces that would encourage openness and creativity as well as distributing leadership. Employees could engage and partake in strategic thinking and, in doing so, subvert anything that was getting in the way of change and collaboration. It also encouraged staff to bring their authentic selves to the process.

Lynne attended these forums to legitimize them and openly participate. The structure of each forum was an evening and a day with space for reflection, communication, and cross-fertilization of ideas. It was stated clearly that whatever role individuals and teams played, their contribution was valuable, and their ideas could make a difference that mattered. The major purpose at this stage was not just to create a strategic plan but to provide the context for new strategies to emerge.

Three key themes emerged from these efforts to democratize strategy:

1. Distributed leadership—this went beyond rhetoric as change initiatives were suggested from all parts of the organization. Together these formed an emergent strategy, particularly in relation to improving processes, communication, and sustaining social networks.
2. Identifying what is sustainable success—there was a shift from the struggle for survival and reactive management to being able to consider a more innovative and brighter future. This was the greatest success produced by the strategic forums.
3. Designing and adapting business models that worked for the whole of CEL—structural and process decisions were made that addressed CEL as a whole rather than individual parts or silos.

As the significant investment in staff development continued, staff strategic forums became embedded, and staff retreats became more powerful, creative, and collective. Junior staff were encouraged to step up into leadership roles.

Simultaneously, Lynne and her team spent extensive time and effort to strengthen relationships with key stakeholders through a mix of relationship building, consultation, and sharing of information. It was always Lynne's intention to ensure that the sector felt that they were the "owners" of CEL, if not literally, then in terms of moral purpose, influence over services, and portfolio development. During this period Lynne gave many presentations to key stakeholders to share the vision and purpose of CEL and to gain feedback to co-create the nature of services desired and to foster engagement with CEL staff. She and her team also established several CEL stakeholder support groups with a range of different functions to meet stakeholder needs and expectations.

A CEL stakeholder advisory group had been established to provide the senior leadership team with input for the development of CEL's portfolio and services. It also made suggestions on the leadership needs of CEL customers. This advisory group was also used successfully to lobby for more public funds.

CEL held developmental meetings with customer stakeholders, who offered advice on what leadership programs and services they felt were most relevant. This ensured creative solutions such as online learning tool kits for the small and medium sized businesses who found it hard to release staff. Leadership modules were developed for the specific needs of different stakeholder groups, as were costs and modes of delivery.

This period illustrates the exercise of Lynne's personal and organizational leadership (Fry & Nisiewicz, 2013). Her work with her coach strengthened her inner life, which helped her renew her hope/faith in her personal vision of service to her staff, clients, and other key stakeholders through altruistic love (Figure 5.2). This gave her a sense of enhanced calling and renewed purpose to make a difference and for her life to have meaning. She also found a renewed sense of membership in her commitment to create a CEL culture where all (including herself) would belong and feel understood and appreciated. Finally, by satisfying these needs for spiritual wellbeing, Lynne felt a renewed personal commitment to CEL, became more centered and productive in her approach to her work, and experienced higher levels of psychological wellbeing and life satisfaction.

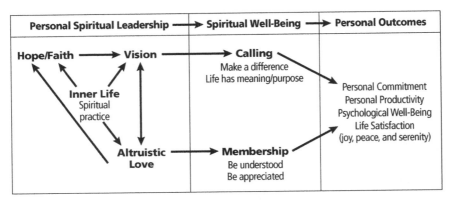

Figure 5.2 Personal spiritual leadership.

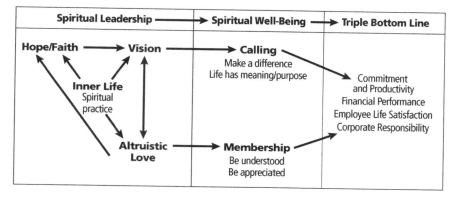

Figure 5.3 Model of organizational spiritual leadership.

Relative to organizational spiritual leadership (Figure 5.3), Lynne began to create an organizational context that would consciously nourish the inner life of all who worked at CEL. On away days, staff worked extremely hard on key work matters; employees also had opportunities for creative expression and collective team work. This included African drumming, verbally hurling Shakespearian insults in alliterative words from Shakespeare's plays with the Royal Shakespeare Company, working with trained actors on professional work issue role plays, salsa dancing, outward bound activities, quizzes, bonfire evenings, and sharing appreciation exercises. They were exciting, energizing and always held huge surprises. In addition, all staff were provided access to a coach or mentor with an annual staff budget of £4,500 per person, a much higher investment in people than the then national benchmark of £300 per person per year spent in universities. This reinforced CEL's core principle that a leadership development center should invest in its employees' inner lives and model positive staff development, especially if, as in CEL's case, an adequate surplus was being generated and performance targets met or exceeded. There was also the introduction of enhanced annual staff retreats to deal with difficult and unspoken issues.

During some of these activities, external facilitators were used to enhance and support team processes. This served to create and reinforce both organizational and staff personal spiritual leadership through hope/faith in CEL's vision and values of caring (altruistic love) and service to key stakeholders. This spiritual leadership process then had a positive effect on employee spiritual wellbeing by creating an enhanced sense of calling and making them feel that their lives had meaning and they made a difference in the lives of others. It also positively affected staffs' sense of membership in that they felt understood and appreciated and part of a community that could openly engage in dialogue. This ultimately fueled higher levels of employee commitment and life satisfaction, a renewed sense of corporate social responsibility, and even higher levels of financial performance.

With the support, understanding, and participation of FE leaders and CEL's vision and values, Lynne instigated a massive external program for FE member engagement for consultation and dialogue and production of new programs and services. During this period, she gave 64 presentations in nine months and formed formal partnerships with 22 FE organizations. Each partner was given clear business and performance goals. Her team also ensured maximum profile and engagement with leaders in the sector.

By initiating these activities and programs, Lynne demonstrated that the full engagement of staff in developing creative ideas, innovation, and the overall strategic direction of CEL was critical for CEL to achieve its goal of self-sufficiency. She knew that the key to CEL's success was the appointment of high performing, highly dedicated staff at all levels and in every function. It was widely acknowledged among FE organizations that poor staff performance was not dealt with swiftly or toughly enough. This was not the case in CEL. CEL created a rigorous individual performance and bonus program to reward high performance that included rewards for understanding of and adherence to the values and culture of the organization. Employees that were high performers could not gain top rewards if their behavior was not supportive of the vision and cultural values of CEL. Anyone who did not "fit" the culture or who underperformed was dealt with through peer pressure or fairly and supportively through the relevant capability and disciplinary procedures. Although some staff left CEL feeling that the culture did not suit them, or that they should have been treated differently, many reported in exit interviews stories of how CEL had impacted positively on their lives and how the wide range of individuals in CEL had made a huge difference to them as professionals and as human beings.

Gradually, cultural misfits and low performers were encouraged and supported to leave (with love, practical advice, dignity, and help in finding a place where they might be a better fit and therefore be more successful). High performing employees were retained and new high quality staff hired. They were all encouraged to co-create role changes and/or additions to their jobs that really interested and inspired them. Initiatives became bottom-up, as well as top-down. CEL was now coming into its own as a trusted and effective organization. The fractious relationship with government had been repaired, and the FE sector believed CEL was beginning to work in its interest. Minister of Skills, Bill Rammell was highly supportive of CEL, and senior civil servants also gave their strong support to ensure CEL's success.

Many partnerships were now in place, and many more participants were completing programs with high customer satisfaction ratings. A new pledge and promise was made publicly that the "new" CEL from March 2006 on would move beyond the original partnership and be the kind of organization FE had always wanted.

For the 2006–2007 fiscal year, CEL exceeded its business plan target by 46%. Initially, the government had set goals of 75% customer satisfaction, 1,500 participants and a breakeven budget for the first three years. During this period, CEL achieved 97% customer satisfaction, 12,000 participants and realized a £1.4m surplus.

Conclusion

As we discussed in Chapters 2 and 3, developing personal and organizational spiritual leadership requires a commitment to the spiritual journey—a journey of transformation to become less ego-centered and more other-centered in striving to fulfill one's ultimate purpose through love and service of others. This entails cultivating an ongoing inner life practice to nurture personal and organizational spiritual leadership. It also requires a supportive spiritual community and can involve working with a spiritual coach or mentor. All three are important to provide regular feedback and counsel concerning the motives of any proposed action and to guard against spiritual pride and to keep reflecting on whether one's service to others is authentic or is about satisfying the ego's own selfish needs and desires.

Lynne Sedgmore discovered early on as CEO of CEL that the spiritual journey is never finished. There is no final destination. In spite of her many years of inner work and seeking to develop her personal spiritual leadership and the successes she had in previous jobs, another "dark night of the soul" appeared that signaled the need for further personal and organizational spiritual leadership development. Her spiritual journey was not over. It now required a renewed commitment to uncover more of her worldly attachments, identifications, and personality fixations. Unless she embraced this invitation, she might get stuck and be unable to surrender to the spiritual lessons presented by current circumstances.

This recognition led her to choose an experienced executive coach who could also serve as a sponsor and spiritual guide as she worked to further cultivate her personal and organizational spiritual leadership. As their work together unfolded, Lynne found herself emerging from this dark night of the soul with a new sense of transformation. This transformation radically changed her view of leadership to one that was more flexible, authentic, and inclusive. Whereas her approach in her previous jobs had been to explore the place of spiritual leadership and workplace spirituality within a traditional bureaucratic organizational environment, she found that a different organizational form and approach was needed for a new venture startup like CEL. The challenge now was to embrace her personal spiritual journey and use it as a springboard for maximizing the triple bottom line through spiritual leadership, regardless of the nature of the organization or its environment.

Based on her work with Dr. Simon Western and his THINK coaching framework for personal and organizational spiritual leadership development, Lynne's initial efforts to democratize strategy and implement the model of organizational spirituality within CEL produced encouraging results. The strategic forums she initiated encouraged distributed leadership among staff, began the process of co-creating a vision of sustainable success, and produced a new learner-focused CEL organizational form. Lynne and her top team's subsequent actions further illustrate the model of organizational spirituality (Figure 1.1) and models of personal and organizational spiritual leadership. In the next chapter we further explore the results of Lynne Sedgmore's effort to introduce workplace spirituality and organizational spiritual leadership throughout CEL, which led to international recognition through the Spirit at Work Award.

Practical Tools

For those interested in implementing spiritual leadership to maximize the triple bottom line, the major tools introduced in this chapter include:

1. *An executive coach and spiritual guide*—Serves as a sponsor that can assist with personal growth in personal spiritual leadership and support professional development of organizational spiritual leadership.
2. *"THINK" coaching*—A framework that may be used to for personal and spiritual leadership development and democratizing strategy through spiritual leadership.

6

The Spirit at Work Award

In October 2007, CEL won the International Spirit at Work Award (CEL receives International Spirit at Work Award, 2007). CEL was only the second UK organization at the time, after the iconic Body Shop, to be honored with this prestigious award for its work to create a new paradigm for organizational performance—one that values wellbeing, social justice, spiritual development, and sustainability as much as business output and material wealth, in short, the triple bottom line. One of seven organizations to be honored at the 2007 annual International Spirit at Work Conference, CEL received the award for its programs on organizational spirituality and its commitment to spiritual leadership with its focus on reflective practice. At that time Lynne stated, "Our commitment to exploring, articulating, and living spiritual values is reflected not only in our leadership development programs but also in our whole approach to staff support and development."

Spiritual Leadership in Action, pages 71–84
Copyright © 2013 by Information Age Publishing

CEL—An Exemplar of Personal and Organizational Spiritual Leadership

Organizations committed to organizational spirituality and spiritual leadership embark on a spiritual journey much the same as that experienced by leaders who commit to the spiritual journey. CEL's submission for the Spirit at Work Award provides a snapshot for just how far CEL had traveled on this journey.

CEL's Vision and Mission, Philosophy, and Core Values

The vision and mission of CEL was focused on the FE leaders CEL serves and the students who learn within their 400 educational colleges and 2,000 training providers. CEL's staff were committed to future generations and to co-creating a better world for all through their contribution to educational leaders in the learning and skills sector of England.

Lynne's underpinning philosophy of leadership was one that embraced spiritual leadership as a collective and relational activity that goes beyond the classic leadership model of the lone, charismatic, egoic hero. Her approach to spiritual leadership had moral purpose at its core and a strong sense of service while encouraging a student- and staff-centered, empowering style that enabled and allowed everyone to develop to their fullest potential.

The CEL board made a clear strategic statement to all staff that "growth is primarily for service not for profits," although they made clear that surpluses were welcome and should flow from true high quality service. CEL's model of spiritual leadership included the intellectual, physical, social, emotional, and spiritual dimensions. Spirituality was exercised in a very broad, pluralistic manner within CEL, and this incorporated both the horizontal dimension (relating to living beings and nature—primarily outwardly focused) and the vertical dimension (transpersonal or theistic—primarily inner focused). As a public sector organization funded by the then Secretary of State for Education, CEL's focus was primarily on the horizontal dimension. This provided the foundation and impetus for vertical discussions, explorations, and discourse to emerge naturally and organically.

Horizontal Dimension of Spirituality

At CEL there was a wide range of de facto definitions and approaches to spirituality. Indeed any other way would not fit with CEL's pluralist and inclusive vision and cultural values. Rather than define spirituality, CEL's approach was to encourage and allow each person to explore, clarify, articulate, and understand his or her own spiritual way of being within CEL and within his or her whole life. For CEL the workplace was a space where spiritual expression, flow, and consciousness were as vital as every other aspect of life.

In this context the horizontal dimension of spirituality speaks to issues of how spirituality is addressed within the organization. CEL was staffed with highly creative, articulate, autonomous individuals with a desire to serve. Conversations about one's soul needs, personal fulfillment, and spiritual aspirations were common. There was no desire by CEO Lynne Sedgmore or the senior team to control or monitor such exchanges.

A structured discourse on the horizontal dimension was encouraged through a values clarification process. With the aid of an external facilitator, Dr. Ann Limb, these were debated, articulated, and agreed upon using a range of staff focus groups, forums, questionnaires, away days, and formal meetings. This collective approach modeled CEL's core value of partnership and collaboration.

CEL also modeled the value of being diverse by truly celebrating and respecting differences while embracing the unity and harmony of the spiritual values that underlie CEL's vision. As part of this effort, CEL produced and launched, in the East London Mosque, the *Faith Communities Toolkit* to assist sector leaders in understanding different faith traditions and belief systems. It was highly popular, with over one thousand copies requested in the first three months of publication. The toolkit was strongly supported and endorsed by faith groups and by the Minister for Further and Higher Education as well as a wide range of well known national interfaith leaders.

The range of spiritual approaches and practices favored and practiced by staff included agnostics, atheists, individuals who might be defined as "new age," and green spirituality, as well as followers of orthodox faith traditions. CEL employed and welcomed openly self-defined agnostics and atheists. To acknowledge all belief systems and to make it clear that CEL did not advocate only religious or spiritual affiliation, the *Faith Communities Toolkit* included definitions for agnosticism and atheism (Center for Excellence in Leadership, 2005).

Agnosticism. Agnosticism is a concept, not a religion. It is a belief related to the existence or non-existence of God. The term "agnosticism" was coined by Professor T. H. Huxley at a meeting of the Metaphysical Society in 1876. He defined an agnostic as someone who disclaimed both atheism and theism, who believed that the question of whether a higher power existed was unsolved and insoluble. An agnostic is a person who feels that God's existence can neither be proved nor disproved on the basis of current evidence. Agnostics note that theologians and philosophers have for millennia tried to prove either that God exists or that God does not exist. None have convincingly succeeded. An agnostic usually holds the question of the existence of God open, pending the arrival of more evidence. They are willing to change their belief if some solid evidence or logical proof is found in the future. However, some have taken the position that there is no logical way in which the existence or the non-existence of a deity can be proven.

Atheism. Atheism is confined to one factor: the existence or non-existence of a deity. Atheism can be the positive belief that there is no deity or it can be the absence of a belief that there is a deity. This absence of belief generally comes about either through deliberate choice or from an inherent inability to believe religious teachings. It is not a lack of belief born out of simple ignorance of religious teachings. Some atheists go beyond a mere absence of belief in gods: they actively believe that particular gods, or all gods, do not exist. Just lacking belief in God or gods is often referred to as the "weak atheist" position; whereas believing that God does not (or cannot) exist is known as "strong atheism."

An atheist will have a personal moral code. However, it is generally derived from secular considerations and not from a "revealed" religious text. Most atheists follow many of the same "moral rules" as theists, but for different reasons. Atheists view morality as something created by humans, according to the way humans feel the world ought to work, rather than seeing it as a set of rules decreed by a supernatural being. Many atheists live a purposeful life and behave in a "moral" or "compassionate" way simply because they feel a natural tendency to empathize with other humans. They decide what gives meaning to life, and they pursue those goals. They try to make their lives count, not by wishing for eternal life, but by having an influence on other people who will live on. For example, an atheist may dedicate his/her life to political reform in the hope of leaving her/his mark on history. Ideas that atheists may promote include:

- There is more to moral behavior than simply following rules.
- Be especially skeptical of positive claims.
- If you want your life to have some sort of meaning, it's up to you to find it.
- Search for what is true, even if it makes you uncomfortable.
- Make the most of your life, as it's probably the only one you'll have.
- It's no good relying on some external power to change you; you must change yourself.
- Just because something's popular doesn't mean it's good.
- If you must assume something, assume something easy to test.

- Don't believe things just because you want them to be true.
- All beliefs should be open to question.

The above descriptions of the beliefs of agnostics and atheists taken from the Faith Communities Toolkit reflect the same spiritual values of love and service that underlie all spiritual and religious traditions. As such this allowed for both to feel welcome as valued employees of CEL contributing to the wide faith and diverse cultural values umbrella that characterized CEL.

Vertical Dimension of Spirituality

Lynne, board member Ann Limb, and several staff members were very open about the vertical, or inward, dimension of spirituality and the centrality of this within their lives. This allowed for an open discourse of the vertical dimension. Inevitably, amid the cultural values debate, vertical dimension questions concerning spiritual and religious practices had emerged. The vertical dimension was made possible through individual coaching (all staff were entitled to a personal development coach), a voluntary program of exploring the Enneagram, and the Dignity at Work training days. Lynne, as the CEO, talked openly about the significance of the vertical dimension in her life and gave time to any member of staff approaching her on this aspect of workplace spirituality.

CEL made the *Faith Communities Toolkit* freely available to all staff, and consequently many staff engaged to a greater or lesser degree with Lynne on the vertical dimension as well as among themselves; this was respected as private unless voluntarily offered by the individual. The vertical dimension was also openly expressed by staff who offered sessions to other staff on yoga, meditation, and massage; on staff away days the vertical dimension was encouraged through venues in beautiful surroundings, often with spa facilities and sufficient space for staff to nurture themselves and to reflect as they chose.

Implementing Spirit at Work

As part of the values dialog, CEL was explicit about diversity, including gender, ethnicity, sexual orientation, age, disability, and faith (Centre for Excellence in Leadership, 2006c). As CEL's offices were based in London— a multicultural, highly diverse city—it attracted people of many different faiths and of no faith. For those who have difficulty or are resistant to bringing their personal spirituality or faith into the workplace, faith, spirituality and religion are placed within the context of diversity—in particular the UK Religious Discrimination Act.

Diversity awareness training was mandatory for all staff and included space to explore all facets of diversity. Through this training, staff gained an understanding of the context and implications of the UK Religious Discrimination Act. They were counseled that disrespecting other faiths and attempting to "correct" inappropriately were not acceptable within the organization. Yet the emphasis—in line with CEL's values—was always to hold this discourse in a respectful manner to enable people, with trained facilitators, to work though their prejudices and biases. The diversity training was explicitly designed to do this and was supported by the CEL "Dignity at Work" (2006c) policy. Staff could not choose to opt out of the diversity training, yet in every other aspect of their own personal faith or spirituality they were free to engage or not, as long as the organizational values were lived and respected.

The values and culture of CEL encouraged open and free expression of who you truly are as a person of faith or no faith. In CEL's open plan office, all kinds of spiritual symbols were evidenced; the hijab was worn, as was crucifix jewelry. A Buddhist Tara sat on a desk next to staff who openly expressed their atheism or agnosticism. It was also accepted that spirituality could be manifested outside of traditional religion, through nature, environmental concerns, and service to others.

During its existence, CEL had few formal complaints or serious concerns in the faith and spirituality arena although everyone had access to the company's complaint and grievance procedures. Part of the reason for this may be due to the discussions that took place on the Dignity at Work days and the fact that CEL was highly diverse, with tolerant staff from over 10 countries and a wide range of ethnicities. Many had worked overseas and traveled widely to different countries and cultures. Collectively, CEL employees spoke over 15 languages.

Clear guidelines were set for acceptable and desirable behavior in CEL. As an example of how CEL was proactive in attempting to foresee and prevent disharmony, we offer an extract from CEL's (2006c) Dignity at Work policy:

> CEL is determined to create a harmonious working and learning environment for all its employees and will not accept any form of behavior that contradicts this principle. CEL accepts that, as a consequence of the Dignity at Work Principle, the dignified treatment of all will involve:

- Eliminating discriminatory practices and guaranteeing equal treatment and opportunity irrespective of gender, marital status, sexual orientation, age, race, color, religious conviction, disability, membership or non-membership of a trade union
- Not accepting behavior that undermines an employee's self esteem, confidence or mental health

CEL does not tolerate behavior that constitutes discrimination, victimization, bullying or harassment in any form, and all staff will undergo mandatory training and education in the principles of Equality, Diversity and Dignity at Work.

Employees are free to express themselves as they choose, and no form of spirituality is excluded from the organization so long as behavior does not discriminate against or harass others. (p. 6)

Overall Approach to Programs and Services

All programs and services were personalized and designed to meet the customer where they were, both accepting where they were in their own developmental journey and working in partnership to co-create and generate creative solutions and improvement.

Explicit spiritual language was not used unless considered relevant to the context. What was made explicit was that CEL facilitated building self-esteem, confidence, critical reflection, self awareness, emotional intelligence, and authentic integrity in leaders at all organizational levels. CEL also encouraged leaders to articulate their own values and moral purpose. Although not made explicit, many of these activities were, in practice, key spiritual and ethical qualities that manifest on the horizontal dimension of spirituality. Facilitators and coaches were aware of occasions when individuals experienced vertical dimensions on CEL's programs, but these were private and confidential unless the individual chose to share.

A "Spirited Leadership" introductory workshop shared the design of a nine day pilot program to model a calm and centered state of being, being present, and the becomingness of the leader. Experiential exercises including visualization, meditation, and silence were offered to develop the key skills of storytelling, deep inquiry, and presence. The workshop was marketed as a new initiative in advanced leadership development to encourage dialogue on leadership purpose, potency, and presence in the sector.

CEL Policies, Programs, or Practices

CEL had the full range of policies expected of a nationally funded government agency. Its wide range of programs, interventions, and services included:

- leadership programs for individuals;
- a tailored organizational consultancy service;
- coaching, mentoring, and careers services;
- national succession, talent management, sustainability, and diversity strategies and services;
- policy seminars and thought documents;
- national conferences (8 per year);
- original research into FE leadership practices and theory; and
- toolkits and e-learning programs.

One example was the "CEL Quality Improvement Policy," which expressed CEL's desire to release energy and innovation while building systems that would satisfy increased scrutiny by funders (Centre for Excellence in Leadership, 2007b). It had a section entitled "Quality Spirit and Aspirations—Approach Based on Values," which expressed the view that "quality is energy" rather than just a procedure and that everything undertaken needs to be infused with a spirit and essence of quality. It talked about the aspiration to build on the "joy in achieving excellence" and how everyone who engaged in CEL's quality procedures and with the CEL portfolio would be "inspired, stretched, supported, challenged, affirmed, intrigued and eager for more." Within this "spirit and energy" of excellence, the policy provided a rigorous process for integrating the hard and soft features of quality into organizational life.

CEL programs for staff development comprised individual, team, and whole community events and approaches. This included access to a coach for personal and professional development. All staff were offered two two-day corporate away days and two one-day strategic forums per year in addition to numerous internal events and external activities relevant to their personal career development plan. Every employee received an annual achievement review where they could receive an annual cost of living and bonus payment of up to 6% each year. This was generous within the sector, as annual average increases were 2 to 3%.

Staff shared their own stories and passions with others as part of staff development events. They shared also their creativity and sponsored workshops in knitting, salsa dancing, hand massage, and poetry. In the annual staff away days, the planning team, led by the HR manager, Lyn Baldwin, included three key dimensions: enhancing team effectiveness and spirit, nourishing creativity and the soul, and facilitating the "stepping into leadership" of junior staff. Venues offered beautiful ground settings to allow nourishing, walking, and reflective space. The feedback from staff away days were outstanding in all three areas.

Lynne took a direct interest in staff development and proactively intervened to encourage and enable the vertical dimension in staff development. At the opening of each strategic senior management team meeting, the team "connected" by sharing personal thoughts, experiences, how they were feeling in that moment, and whatever else arose. The business element of the meeting built on this space of deep personal sharing.

CEL recognized the value of storytelling and produced many case studies and stories of customer experience and success. It encouraged staff to share their own stories. Leaders from the sector were treated as wise elders and sat on advisory groups to share their learning experience and wisdom.

Reflection and Self-awareness

CEL considered the need for critical self-reflection and awareness as central to all its programs for customers and its own development of staff. Indeed one of CEL's values was "We are reflective practitioners continually improving our professionalism and seeking feedback." A range of 360° diagnostic tools was used, including GELI, MBTI, Facet 24, the Enneagram, and the CEL Leadership Qualities Framework. Emotional and spiritual intelligence were viewed as key components of leadership effectiveness. Overall this eclectic and diverse approach encouraged a huge appetite and choice from staff, most of whom were keen and willing to engage; most staff members engaged in their own structured self awareness activity at some point in their employment with CEL.

Customer Feedback

CEL proactively sought feedback from customers. Every program had an evaluation process that provided evidence of program effectiveness, and feedback was highly positive. Representative comments include:

> All participants had gained something from the program and had begun to implement learning at both a personal and professional level.

> Impact is occurring at largely a personal, managerial and collaborative level but over time, noticeable positive impacts have occurred beyond these levels.

> ... significant impact ... certainly achieved the objectives of enabling us [the senior managers] to reflect upon our current practice, to identify the ways in which we worked individually and as teams and therefore to work much better as a team and I think most of us felt that our individual skills improved as a result of that process of reflection, analysis and debate and the work with the consultants.

> CEL has done a lot for the FE sector overall: professionalization of training programs; E&D agenda—providers more reflective of community ethnic mix. Must do more but has made a good start.

In addition, CEL produced over 20 case studies endorsed by clients that provided narratives of how they felt CEL supported and enhanced their leadership and organizational performance. The one below highlights growth in self-awareness:

> The signposting day was one of the most exhilarating things I have done in terms of assessment. It went through my strengths and weaknesses, about how we perceive ourselves, and I found it remarkably accurate. I learnt a lot about myself.

CEL's 2006/2007 portfolio was full of direct quotes from named satisfied customers. Samples include:

> It's been exhilarating and has given me a new outlook on my future. I now know that I'm capable of doing more and have set my sights higher. I've also promoted the course to colleagues.

> When I went back to work after my first day on the course, my colleagues were amazed at how I knew about what was going on in FE because I am such a little person in the college. The course has made me tall.

> I gained an immense amount from the program and was able to maintain my learning, reflection and development back at work. Thanks again for the support and guidance.

The Further Education Sector

By March 2007, less than four years after its launch, CEL had trained nearly 26,000 individual participants and worked with 91% of the organizations in the learning and skills system. CEL's annual review of that period shows that 12,000 participants were recruited during the financial year to

March 31, 2007, exceeding the target by 46%, and that customer satisfaction had improved again, with 97% of participants rating CEL's programs, courses, or events as good or very good.

In March 2007, CEL published the results of an independent review by the Oakleigh Consulting Group, *CEL's Impact in the FE Sector* (Oakleigh Consulting Group, 2007, p. 7). The report established the strong impact that CEL interventions have had on individuals, organizations, learners, the wider environment, and the FE sector as a whole. The review gathered evidence from interviews and an e-survey that targeted senior sector leaders, participants in CEL programs, CEL's own program evaluations, and other key stakeholders. Key findings included:

- convincing evidence that CEL was having a strong and positive impact on the further education sector;
- CEL had been a significant catalyst for change;
- CEL had focused the debate about leadership, management, governance, and diversity issues within the FE sector;
- CEL had a direct effect on individuals and on institutions;
- There was evidence that these impacts will in turn have a beneficial effect on learners;
- CEL's reflective and learning approach provided a model to the rest of the sector;
- CEL had gained a high reputation within the sector;
- CEL's programs were recognized as being relevant to the sector; and
- Research was a key area, providing an intelligence-led approach to program design (Oakleigh Consulting Group, 2007).

The summary concludes by saying:

We can say with a high degree of certainty that CEL, in its first years of operation, has justified its creation and lived up to the expectations within the sector. It has raised awareness of key management and leadership issues in the sector and provided at least partial solutions. (Oakleigh Consulting Group, 2007, p. ?)

CEL as an Exemplar of the Model of Organizational Spirituality and Spiritual Leadership

CEL had established itself as a champion, with leading edge practice in diversity and by being at the leading edge of leadership development while including the spiritual and faith dimension of leadership. It was an unusual and, perhaps, courageous thing to have been explicit about the spiritual dimension of leadership within the public sector leadership arena. At the time there were 15 public sector leadership centers within the UK, and no other center had developed explicit work on leadership and faith or such a comprehensive approach to the spiritual dimension of leadership.

CEL became a model of good practice in organizational spirituality (Figure 1.1) and in spiritual leadership (Figure 3.1) for other organizations by:

- producing the first national *Faith Communities Toolkit* for leaders;
- sponsoring a national review on "Making Space for Faith" in the learning and skills sector;
- piloting the "Spirited Leadership" program;
- investing an average of £4,700 per member of staff annually;
- introducing an annual achievement bonus scheme closely aligned to values and diversity as well as performance;
- holding events in creative, inspirational, and unusual venues;
- researching and benchmarking itself on both traditional HR performance criteria and on the spiritual dimension;
- having endorsement from the Prime Minister in its 2006/2007 annual review; and
- introducing an innovative staff questionnaire on spirituality and wellbeing.

CEL had established itself as the national agency willing to champion faith and spirituality as a vital part of the FE education curriculum and as a key aspect of the work of college leaders. CEL had developed a strong partnership with the National Ecumenical Agency of Further Education (NEAFE) to establish CEL as a key source of leadership and faith knowledge, support, and advice to UK Ministers, particularly to Bill Rammell, Minister of Further Education and Higher Education who was also the government's minister for multi-faith matters. He held CEL in high regard as was evidenced by his public comments and personal launch of its publications and his frequent attendances at CEL's national events. CEL also supported, sponsored, and advised NEAFE on the initiation and implementation of a national inquiry into the opportunity for spiritual and moral development across learning and skills entitled "Making Space for Faith."

In addition, Lynne Sedgmore as CEO was widely recognized for developing a model of organizational spirituality and for practicing both personal and organizational spiritual leadership. She gave national keynote speeches and facilitated workshops and "conversations" for Surrey University, the St Ethelburga's Centre, NEAFE and the United Nations. She chaired the UK Interfaith Seminary and published four articles sharing her experiences and views on spirituality.

Conclusion

CEO Lynne Sedgmore, together with CEL's board and her top management team, led CEL on a spiritual journey along the organizational spirituality and spiritual leadership models' paths that challenged staff to develop their own personal spiritual leadership. CEL's approach was to encourage and allow everyone to explore, clarify, articulate, and act on their own spiritual way of being within CEL and to discover how that understanding could support their lives, especially at work.

CEL's vision of service to key stakeholders based on a culture centered in altruistic love provided the foundation and benchmark for both the horizontal and vertical dimensions of spirituality, which worked to support a wide range of approaches to spirituality and religion within CEL. Through its commitment to reflection and self-awareness; innovative approach to programs, policies, practices, and services; and its proactive pursuit for customer feedback, CEL became recognized as a model of excellence for leadership development in the learning and skills sector.

The UK public sector does not have a tradition of accepting and supporting workplace spirituality. Receiving the Spirit at Work Award gave CEL international recognition as an organization that had developed a model of organizational spirituality to implement workplace spirituality based on personal and organizational leadership. The next chapter will provide further evidence that CEL was a high performance organization that maximized the triple bottom line.

Practical Tools

For those interested in implementing spiritual leadership to maximize the triple bottom line, the major tools introduced in this chapter include:

1. *The model of organizational spirituality* (See Chapter 1)—Provides the broader organizational context and necessary components for implementing spiritual leadership.
2. *The personal spiritual leadership model* (See Chapter 2)—Provides a roadmap for personal leadership based on a vision of service to others through altruistic love to maximize spiritual wellbeing and,

ultimately, personal commitment and productivity, psychological wellbeing, and life satisfaction.

3. *The organizational spiritual leadership model* (See Chapter 3)—Provides a roadmap for implementing organizational spiritual leadership based on a vision of service to key stakeholders through altruistic love to maximize the triple bottom line.

7

Spiritual Leadership in Action

In receiving the Spirit at Work award, CEL gained international recognition for its application of spirituality in the workplace. We believe that CEL during this period was also demonstrating spiritual leadership in action. This chapter will go into more detail in terms of the organizational spiritual leadership model's inner workings and the actual management practices that CEL used to implement and sustain it.

The foundation for implementing the organizational spiritual leadership model is built around several principles. First, employee involvement and commitment are the most effective sources of control. Involvement and commitment create intrinsic controls because the employees have a sense of ownership, and they focus their energy and creativity on the improvement of organizational processes and the attainment of organizational objectives. When employees are involved and committed to their work, they add significant value to the organization.

Second, a spiritual organization utilizes team-based work designs. Team-based approaches to organizing should be centered on issues relating to products and customers rather than the traditional functions of the

Spiritual Leadership in Action, pages 85–101
Copyright © 2013 by Information Age Publishing
All rights of reproduction in any form reserved.

organization. This is also necessary to implement organizational spiritual leadership as a driver of the spiritual leadership balanced scorecard business model to maximize the triple bottom line, which we cover for CEL in detail in the next chapter.

Third, leaders work to identify emerging organizational issues and to interact with frontline employees to get a feel for how decisions are being implemented and to learn about any unintended side effects. Leaders also serve as role models for the rest of the organization to develop a culture that is comfortable with identifying failures and using them as opportunities for organizational learning.

Implementing Organizational Spiritual Leadership

The process for implementing organizational spiritual leadership to address these three issues is illustrated in Figure 7.1. The source of spiritual leadership is a set of leader and management practices that support employee inner life and provide the source for hope/faith in a vision of service to key stakeholders based in altruistic love. The vision (what is our journey), purpose (why this journey is important), and mission (what we employees do to fulfill our purpose as we engage in our vision quest) work together in synergy with key stakeholders.

It is through being committed to a vision grounded in service to key stakeholders that both leaders and staff develop a sense of calling where they feel they are making a difference in other people's lives and therefore their own lives have meaning and purpose. Employees also develop a sense of membership in being understood, appreciated, and cared for as the organization's leaders "walk the talk" in cultural values and an ethical system

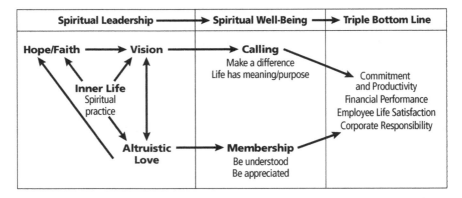

Figure 7.1 Model for implementing organizational spiritual leadership.

based in altruistic love. The combined experiences of calling and membership are the key components of spiritual wellbeing, which then positively influences the triple bottom line.

In the organizational spiritual leadership model, leaders are responsible for creating vision and value congruence across organizational levels as well as developing effective relationships between the organization and environmental stakeholders. To facilitate this congruence, several key ongoing practices are critical for implementing organizational spiritual leadership (see Table 7.1).

First, conduct a periodic assessment of organizational spiritual leadership using the spiritual leadership survey methodology that has been developed and extensively tested by the International Institute for Spiritual Leadership. This survey is used to establish a baseline for the variables in the organizational spiritual leadership model. The survey, usually administered in intervals between 12 and 24 months, also identifies key issues for later organizational transformation and/or development interventions.

The next step, after the establishment of a baseline based on the results of the spiritual leadership survey, is to conduct a vision/stakeholder analysis. This vision/stakeholder analysis, typically initiated by the leadership team, establishes or reinforces the organization's vision, purpose, mission, and cultural values. It explores the key stakeholder issues raised through the spiritual leadership survey for a subsequent organization-wide dialogue concerning the appropriate goals and strategies to address these issues.

TABLE 7.1 Practices for Implementing Spiritual Leadership

- Administer Organizational Spiritual Leadership Survey to establish a baseline and raise key issues.
- Conduct vision/stakeholder analysis
  - Co-Create shared organizational vision/purpose/mission and values.
  - Develop stakeholder effectiveness criteria, issues and goals.
  - Organize and create empowered teams/task forces around key issues.
  - Develop strategy to implement goals through empowered teams.
  - Review/Develop stakeholder information systems to measure effectiveness.
- Conduct organizational development interventions and skills training in:
  - Elements of team empowerment;
  - Collaborative, consensus-based decision making;
  - Managing conflict;
  - Managing and overcoming resistance to change; and
  - Overcoming anger, resentment, and fear through forgiveness, acceptance, and gratitude.
- Align changes with organization design variables, including structure, information technology, production/service technology, promotion and reward systems, and recruiting, selection and training processes.

Third, effectively implementing the organizational spiritual leadership model requires that workers develop basic skills for working in empowered teams, collaborative, consensus-based decision making, and managing conflict and overcoming resistance to change. In addition, it is necessary for them to develop the ability to exercise forgiveness, acceptance, and gratitude to mute the effects of workplace anger, resentment, worry, and fear.

Finally, the organization should focus on aligning key organizational design variables to reinforce any organizational development or change initiatives targeted to address key issues. The basic idea behind organizational design is that there are several key variables—structure, task or work technology, information technology, people, and reward systems—that must fit or be in alignment for an organization to implement its vision, values, goals, and strategies. A change in any one of the design variables will call for adjustments in the others, as they all must form an integrated whole or system. The values that comprise the organization's culture form the glue that holds this system together.

The Research Project

In November 2006, CEL commissioned a two-year research project to examine organizational effectiveness and wellbeing in CEL through an in-depth study of the organization as seen by its principal internal and external stakeholders (given in Figure 5.1). A specific objective of the study was to examine the spiritual essence and leadership of CEL as a non-faith organization that strived to maximize the triple bottom line. The study team was led by Dr. Yochanan Altman and co-researchers Dr. Mustafa Ozbilgin and Dr. Elizabeth Wilson (2007).

This study was informed by the model of organizational spiritual leadership and utilized various qualitative and quantitative methods, including the spiritual leadership survey, which was developed and has been validated in a number of previous studies by Dr. Louis Fry and the International Institute for Spiritual Leadership. The survey study was comprised of two parts. The first survey was administered during and after the winter staff away days in November, 2006. A second survey gathered data in April, 2008.

A major goal was to understand the apparent success of CEL in order to:

- provide insights to organization members about the antecedents for CEL's success and how this momentum could be maintained and further developed;
- provide a platform for reflecting on the future direction of CEL;

- draw lessons (generalizations) applicable to other work organizations and to leadership in general;
- delineate the history, structure, processes and values of CEL as far as they impinged upon and explained the current performance and wellbeing of organization members.

Within this final aim, the following objectives were specified:

- extract models of effectiveness (organizational and personal) from established theory and practice and delineate "good management practice" against which CEL could be assessed;
- explain the contributing internal factors (e.g., values, competencies, processes) and related external factors (e.g., stakeholders) for organizational success and wellbeing and explore their relevance to CEL;
- explore methods for measurement of successful performance and validate the successful performance of CEL against relevant criteria as perceived by organization members;
- explore methods for measurement of wellbeing and validate wellbeing at CEL against relevant criteria as perceived by organization members;
- explicate a model of excellence based on extant knowledge, including the emerging spirituality literature; and
- suggest reflections on CEL in the context of its present performance and future challenges.

Research Stages

A survey methodology with two parallel lines of inquiry was adopted for this study: a "traditional" HR approach, explicating people and organizational processes; and a "new" spirituality approach, examining transpersonal and trans-organizational issues, meaning, and sense-making. The work was conducted in four stages. At each stage there was discussion and consultation with relevant CEL personnel and key stakeholders.

Stage One: Validation of successful performance. The work in the first stage aimed to realize the first objective of the project—validate the successful performance of CEL against relevant criteria as perceived by organization members. It involved multiple parallel activities including participant observation, interviews, group interviews, storytelling sessions, and the study of relevant documentation. These revealed the standards, values, and procedures by which the organization operated.

Stage Two: Internal and external drivers for success. The second stage of the project was built on the first phase of data collection and explored the interplay among internal and external factors contributing to the current and future success of the organization. This stage included administration of the organizational spiritual leadership survey as well as further interviews with relevant stakeholders and participant observation.

Stage Three: Extracting models of effectiveness. Stage Three was designed to extract models of effectiveness (organizational and personal) against established theory and practice. This phase used the data from Stage One to reveal parameters of "good management." It was at this stage that the model of organizational spirituality (Figure 1.1) was developed.

Stage Four: Projecting future performance challenges. The last stage of the project explored future performance challenges at the personal and organizational levels. This part of the project highlighted implications and challenges for CEL against its current mission. This was explored through interviewing a cross-section of organization members as well as examining data from the previous investigations.

Research Methods

To further validate the survey, the study employed a variety of measures including the following.

Interviews. The entire top management of CEL, as well as the chairman of the board and a trustee were interviewed, with 21 interviews in all. Interviews typically lasted an hour, were tailored around the specific role of incumbents, and covered issues such as an assessment of CEL's past and present performance: achievements, deficiencies and challenges, a vision of CEL's future, leadership and organizational culture, relationships with and among stakeholders, as well as personal aspirations. Interviews were taped and transcribed. Additional one-to-one interviews were undertaken of a representative cross-section of CEL's employees and associates as well as a senior civil servant. These were semi-structured interviews, lasting up to an hour, and some were taped and transcribed.

Focus groups. Two focus groups were convened to which CEL core employees and associates were invited to attend and contribute to the study by reflecting on the topic "life in and with CEL." Discussions were guided by key questions, and participants were encouraged to elicit memorable events and characteristic stories.

Targeted participant observation. This included the two internal staff away days for team building in November 2006, a strategic forum in March 2007, a corporate directors' meeting in May 2007, and a discussion forum with clients and associates on the Growing Leadership program (one of CEL's regular programs) in March 2007.

Following pilot testing, the number of background data questions was reduced, as concerns were raised by some that anonymity might be compromised. The questionnaire, its rationale, and purpose were presented at a cross-directorate meeting (a quarterly forum open to all CEL staff) and emailed to all relevant employees and made available on CEL's intranet. Two further reminders were sent over the following three weeks.

Anonymity was assured by requesting respondents to deposit their filled questionnaires in a closed ballot box prominently positioned in the staff room and accessed confidentially by an HR manager. In all 34 filled questionnaires were received (a 54% response rate, which was considered acceptable and representative of the surveyed population).

Respondent demographics were as follows. The largest age group, a third of the total, was 26–30 years old. Most informants (41%) recorded less than one-year employment history with the company. A third held some line management responsibility, and a half classified themselves as non-managers. The data was treated to a singular analysis as no discernable differences were found among the independent variables (the background data questions).

The Spiritual Leadership Survey—Establishing a Baseline

A key aspect of the study was the use of the organizational spiritual leadership survey (Fry, 2008; Fry, Hannah, Noel, & Walumba, 2011; Fry, Matherly, & Ouimet, 2010; Fry, Vitucci, & Cedillo, 2005) based on the work of the authors and the International Institute of Spiritual Leadership (http://www.iispiritualleadership.com/). The survey questionnaire utilized a 1–10 (from Strongly Disagree to Strongly Agree) response set.

Table 7.2 identifies the items used to measure organizational spiritual leadership. To date, the organizational spiritual leadership survey has been extensively tested and validated in a variety of settings. Studies have been conducted in numerous organizations ranging in size from a few employees to over 1,200, including schools, military units, municipalities, the police, and for-profit organizations. These studies have confirmed the spiritual leadership model and its reliability and validity. Results so far support a significant positive influence of organizational spiritual leadership on employee and unit life satisfaction, organizational commitment and productivity, unit performance, sales growth, and corporate social responsibility.

TABLE 7.2 Organizational Spiritual Leadership Survey

Inner Life—the extent to which one has a spiritual practice
1. I feel hopeful about life
2. I consider myself a spiritual person.
3. I care about the spiritual health of my co-workers.
4. I maintain a spiritual practice (e.g., spending time in nature, prayer, meditation, reading inspirational literature, yoga, observing religious traditions, writing in a journal).
5. My spiritual values influence the choices I make.

Hope/Faith—the assurance of things hoped for, the conviction that the organization's vision/purpose/mission will be fulfilled
1. I have faith in my organization and I am willing to "do whatever it takes" to ensure that it accomplishes its mission.
2. I demonstrate my faith in my organization and its mission by doing everything I can to help us succeed.
3. I persevere and exert extra effort to help my organization succeed because I have faith in what it stands for.
4. I set challenging goals for my work because I have faith in my organization and want us to succeed.

Altruistic Love—a sense of wholeness, harmony, and wellbeing produced through care, concern, and appreciation for both self and others
1. The leaders in my organization "walk the walk" as well as "talk the talk."
2. The leaders in my organization are honest and without false pride.
3. My organization is trustworthy and loyal to its employees.
4. The leaders in my organization have the courage to stand up for their people.
5. My organization is kind and considerate toward its workers and, when they are suffering, wants to do something about it.

Meaning/Calling—a sense that one's life has meaning and makes a difference
1. The work I do makes a difference in people's lives.
2. The work I do is meaningful to me.
3. The work I do is very important to me.
4. My job activities are personally meaningful to me.

Membership—a sense that one is understood and appreciated
1. I feel my organization appreciates me and my work.
2. I feel my organization demonstrates respect for me and my work.
3. I feel I am valued as a person in my job.
4. I feel highly regarded by my leaders.

Organizational Commitment—the degree of loyalty or attachment to the organization
1. I feel like "part of the family" in this organization.
2. I really feel as if my organization's problems are my own.
3. I would be very happy to spend the rest of my career with this organization.
4. I talk up this organization to my friends as a great place to work for.
5. I feel a strong sense of belonging to my organization.

Productivity—efficiency in producing results, benefits, or profits
1. In my department, everyone gives his/her best efforts.
2. In my department, work quality is a high priority for all workers.
3. My work group is very productive.
4. My work group is very efficient in getting maximum output from the resources (money, people, equipment, etc.) we have available.

(continued)

TABLE 7.2   Organizational Spiritual Leadership Survey (continued)

Satisfaction with Life—one's sense of subjective wellbeing or satisfaction with life as a whole

1. The conditions of my life are excellent.
2. I am satisfied with my life.
3. In most ways my life is ideal.
4. If I could live my life over, I would change almost nothing.
5. So far I have gotten the important things I want in life.

Results of the survey are summarized in Figure 7.2. Given in this figure are the averages for the two survey administrations (November 2006 and April 2008) for inner life, spiritual leadership (vision, hope/faith, and altruistic love), spiritual wellbeing (calling and membership), two learning and growth measures (life satisfaction and organizational commitment), and a measure of unit productivity (other performance measures as they relate to the triple bottom line will be offered in the next chapter). An asterisk denotes that there is a statistically significant difference between averages for the responses on that variable from 2006 to 2008.

The bar graphs depict the dispersion of responses for these measures. Responses between 1.00 and 4.99 represent "Disagree." "Neither" is the percentage of respondents with an average response value between 5.00 and 6.99. The "Agree" percentage represents response values between 7.00 and 10.00. Based on previous experience and research, organizations would want all their employees to have high average response scores (above 7) and report moderately high (above 60%) percentage levels of agreement for all nine variables of the spiritual leadership model. These levels have been found to indicate high levels of spiritual leadership. Moderate or low levels (below 60%) on responses indicate areas for possible intervention for organizational development.

The spiritual leadership research project provided empirical evidence that CEL was a spiritually led organization with high levels of inner life, spiritual leadership, spiritual wellbeing, and organizational commitment and productivity. Averages for all variables except inner life (6.88) were above 7.0 on the final administration. Percent "Agree" responses, with the exception of organizational commitment, were above 60% for both surveys (percentage for organizational commitment in 2006 was 58%). However, organizational commitment saw a significant increase in its average score between surveys, significantly increasing from 5.88 to 7.23 from 2006 to 2008. The researchers believed that this significant increase was most likely due to the ongoing success of the CEL initiatives, based in organizational spiritual leadership, that were implemented during this period.

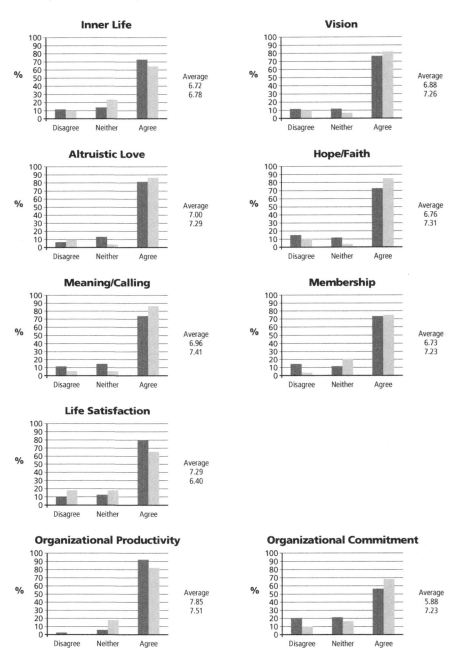

Figure 7.2 Summary of findings from the CEL Organizational Spiritual Leadership Survey.

Vision/Stakeholder Analysis

Chapters 4 and 5 detailed the process through which CEL developed and reinforced its vision of providing world-class educational leadership for every learner in the learning and skills sector of the UK. The stakeholder analysis views organizations as being embedded in layers or levels (individual, group, organizational, societal) with various internal and external constituencies (employees, customers, suppliers, government agencies, and so forth), all of whom have a legitimate strategic and moral stake in the organization's performance. Each of these stakeholders may have different values and interests as well as different stakeholder relationships with other individuals, groups, and organizations.

CEL's key stakeholders fell into five general categories (see figure 5.1). Each of these stakeholders had a set of expectations that CEL had to meet or exceed if it was to be considered a highly effective organization.

- ▪ *Learners*—During its existence nearly 40,000 participants used CEL services, many of whom were repeat learners who attended more than one CEL program. The primary focus of CEL participants was to achieve their own leadership development objectives, and to make a difference within their own organizations as effective leaders. CEL exceeded all participation targets, achieved significant growth, and generated annual surpluses of over £1 million, which it reinvested into new research into leadership and the development and piloting of new cutting-edge programs and organizational development interventions.
- ▪ *Provider organizations*—Second to direct learners, the colleges and organizations that provided the learners for CEL's programs were CEL's main stakeholders. CEL had to keep them happy since they paid for program services and reported back to government Ministers and civil servants if they believed CEL was efficient and effective in its service delivery, or not. These stakeholders consisted of the college principals, chairs of corporations, and other CEOs in the learning and skills sector. They included:
  - – 385 colleges of different types—general further education (GFE) colleges, sixth form colleges, specialist colleges (e.g., for disability or land based), and tertiary colleges;
  - – 2,000 small private training organizations partially funded by the government—these could be very small with six staff or very large with a £30m operating budget and hundreds of staff; and

– adult education and community education in local authorities and other organizations.

▪ *Primary Partners*—Ashridge Business School, Lancaster University Business School, and the LSDA formed the three organizations comprising the original partnership that won the bid to set up a new national leadership center, which eventually evolved into CEL. They were called primary because they had a contractual relationship with CEL to assist CEL's management as well as taking a central role in the development and delivery of key leadership programs.

▪ *Sector Partners*—CEL contracted with other organizations to provide the leadership expertise CEL needed for its training programs and projects. These included national agencies, private companies, and other organizations funded by the government.

▪ *Department of Education and Skills (DfES), Government Agencies, and Key Ministers*—CEL also had to keep relevant government Ministers content with progress in meeting its performance and customer feedback goals. CEL was launched by the Secretary of State and monitored by the Skills Minister. The "Success For All" policy was a government initiative that led to CEL's founding. This initiative focused on improving teaching and learning across the sector and positioned leadership as a core component of improving the standard of teaching and learning.

CEL's Stakeholder Effectiveness

CEL established formal partnerships with over 20 organizations in the UK and delivered leadership development for 12 countries, including Iraq and China. Diversity was core to CEL's mission and services, and in 2004 CEL won the national British Diversity Award for the Black Leadership Initiative project led by Rajinder Mann. CEL was ranked 47th in the Stonewall good employer index in 2006. By the end of the financial year 2007, less than four years after its launch, CEL had recruited nearly 26,000 individual participants and worked with 91% of the organizations in the learning and skills sector (exceeding their target by 46%), and customer satisfaction had improved significantly (96% of participants rating CEL's programs, courses, or events as good or very good).

These achievements were further confirmed by a report from March 2007—*Review of CEL's Impact in the FE Sector.* This report described the strong impact that CEL interventions had on individuals, organizations, learners, the wider environment, and the learning and skills sector as a whole (Centre for Excellence in Leadership, 2007c). This objective review gathered evidence from interviews and an e-survey that targeted senior sector leaders, participants in CEL programs, CEL's own program evaluations, and other key stakeholders. Of interest were the findings that CEL's reflective learning approach provided a model to the rest of the sector and that research was a key in-house value, providing an informative approach to program design and a learning loop for continuous self-improvement. The report concluded:

> We can say with a high degree of certainty that CEL, in its first years of operation, has justified its creation and lived up to the expectations within the sector. It has raised awareness of key management and leadership issues in the sector and provided at least partial solutions. (Centre for Excellence in Leadership, 2007c, p. 15)

Organizational Development Interventions and Skills Training

Organizations wishing to implement the spiritual leadership model should identify areas for improvement and training to implement and sustain the goals and strategies necessary to address key issues. These issues were identified for CEL based on the results from the spiritual leadership survey and the vision stakeholder analysis. This set the stage for CEL's initial organizational development interventions.

Lynne's commitment to democratizing strategy through strategic forums, which was detailed in Chapter 5, illustrates one way organizations can approach initial change and organizational interventions to implement the spiritual leadership model. The forums and staff away days defined a vision/stakeholder analysis process to identify stakeholder issues and develop strategies to address them. This resulted in staff responding with renewed responsibility, accountability, and trust and provided a mechanism to reinforce and encourage staff to step up into leadership roles.

Empowered teams comprising members most affected were then formed to address key issues. As is true for many organizations, a major issue throughout CEL's history was the tendency to work in silos. However, the growing organization and the more complex issues it faced now required cross functional team-based responses.

The elements of empowerment that were implemented for these teams to be effective included:

- teams receiving information about organizational performance,
- employees developing knowledge and skills to contribute to organizational goals,
- employees having the power to make substantive decisions,
- employees understanding the meaning and impact of their jobs, and
- employees rewarded based on both individual and organizational performance.

When CEL moved to a new larger office it was decided collectively to reorganize the seating so that staff were not grouped by function, and senior staff were scattered around the room to reinforce CEL's egalitarian culture.

The bi-annual staff retreats became a forum in which issues could be addressed through activities that fostered team work, the authentic airing of concerns and differences, and new ways of working. Interventions included outward bound activities, African drumming and chanting in harmony, exercises of appreciation, sharing of passions and hobbies, and role plays of real time work dramas. For example, the issue of invoices not being returned to the finance department in time was speeded up by the finance team creating a drumming chant on "getting invoices in on time"—the humor and appeal of this unusual and creative intervention resulted in improved invoice returns.

To generate effective cross organizational systems, staff were trained and supported in management information systems and budget development. A key value of CEL was to empower teams through delegation and transparent information. A balanced scorecard was developed and made available for all to see and comment on. In addition, an internal goal-setting process was introduced by the deputy CEO, Ivor Jones, which involved all staff in setting targets within an open and intelligent debate on any variances. This was at the heart of a goal-setting process that was realistic, challenging, and, most importantly, set by the teams themselves.

A new performance appraisal system was established by the HR team to ensure that staff benefited from CEL's outstanding performance. It was closely aligned to the values of the organization and to performance. Both individual bonuses and a corporate bonus were introduced.

Aligning Changes with Organization Design Variables

These changes must be aligned with key organizational design variables. With the help of Dr. Western, Lynne developed a new CEL organizational structure (Figure 5.1) to create a more organic, less hierarchical organization. In doing so, CEL:

- implemented an organizational design based on self-managed teams and decentralized decision making,
- selectively recruited new personnel who identified with the company's vision and values,
- offered compensation that was contingent upon performance,
- invested heavily in extensive training and development of staff,
- ensured transparency of financial and performance information at every level, and
- reduced positional status distinctions and barriers.

In addition, Lynne discovered that other activities were needed to develop new leaders who could effectively strengthen relationships with key stakeholders. These included further interventions and training on team empowerment; collaborative, consensus-based decision making; managing conflict; managing and overcoming resistance to change; and dealing with workplace anger, resentment and fear through forgiveness acceptance, and gratitude.

An example of an intervention to foster team spirit and empowerment was an exercise in which each member of the staff randomly picked a name from a hat. They then were asked to write an anonymous message of appreciation naming the qualities they admired in that person. At a staff dinner, a certificate of appreciation was put on the seat of each staff member. When people read their personalized appreciation message they were visibly touched by the compliment, but more so since they did not know the identity of the writer. This exercise opened up a collective sense of good feeling and enhanced cohesion throughout the organization.

Expert consultants were brought into CEL to allow space in which staff teams could discuss confidentially issues they were facing internally and or with other teams.

All staff had access to a coach and/or a mentor, which the majority of staff utilized. This provided a safe space to explore one's own issues and contributions to success and problems in CEL and was highly valued by staff.

Where a member of staff did not fit the culture and was unable to work effectively with their team members, open expression of the issues as a peer group was encouraged. Only at the final stage would the HR department intervene with due process and procedures to enable the exit of the individuals involved. It was felt critical that those who did exit did so with dignity and support for future success in their career.

The Dignity at Work training, which all staff were encouraged to attend, assisted greatly in generating a culture of mutual respect, understanding, and respecting both differences and commonalities of faith, gender, ethnicity, and sexual orientation. Staff were equipped to engage in dialogues and conversations that had once felt scary and problematic. This both supplemented and reinforced extra-work sociality among staff members, with numerous social get-togethers, which in turn reinforced team spirit at work.

Conclusion

CEO Lynne Sedgmore and her leadership team exemplify spiritual leadership in action. Through initiating a dialogue that fully involved all staff, CEL constructed its vision of service to key stakeholders based on the values of altruistic love. The central goal, as this process unfolded, was for staff to know, believe in, and become committed to the vision and values of a public service organization that embodied spiritual leadership.

CEL was committed also to analyzing and documenting its path to becoming a high performance organization. The result was to conduct a two-phase research study on organizational effectiveness and wellbeing. This included administering the spiritual leadership survey to all CEL staff in 2006 and 2008, as well as conducting an ongoing vision/stakeholder analysis to establish a baseline and raise key issues.

The combination of the results from the spiritual leadership survey and the vision stakeholder analysis set the stage for CEL's initial change and organizational development interventions. With the help of Dr. Western, Lynne developed a new CEL organizational structure to democratize strategy. This commitment illustrates how organizations can approach initial change interventions to implement the organizational spiritual leadership model through a series of forums to democratize strategy through full engagement of staff.

The strategic forums and staff away days defined a process and created an organizational context that nourished the inner life of CEL workers. It also provided the foundation for team empowerment to identify stakeholder issues and develop strategies to address them, which resulted in staff responding with renewed responsibility, accountability, and trust. Lynne increasingly found that one of her major activities was to develop new leaders who could effectively strengthen relationships with key stakeholders. She then began to use the forums as a mechanism to reinforce and encourage staff to step up into leadership roles.

Overall, CEL achieved a powerful strategic position and significantly influenced its key stakeholders, including national FE educational and leadership policy, while working effectively with senior civil servants, national agencies, and politicians at the ministerial level. CEL did that by creating an entrepreneurial, creative, transparent, and responsive organization using the organizational spiritual leadership model to maximize the triple bottom line.

Practical Tools

For those interested in implementing spiritual leadership to maximize the triple bottom line, the major tools introduced in this chapter include:

1. *The organizational spiritual leadership model*—Provides a roadmap for organizational spiritual leadership based on a vision of service to key stakeholders through altruistic love to maximize spiritual wellbeing and, ultimately, the triple bottom line
2. *Organizational spiritual leadership survey*—Measures the key elements of the organizational spiritual leadership model to raise key issues and provide a baseline for subsequent organizational development, change, and design initiatives
3. *Vision/stakeholder analysis*—Offers a process for implementing and reinforcing the organizational spiritual leadership model by further identifying key stakeholder issues and developing the goals and strategies to address them.

8

CEL

Maximizing the Triple Bottom Line Through Spiritual Leadership

Lynne Sedgmore was intent from the start to make a significant and positive impact on the learning and skills sector by modeling a high performing organization and basing its values and conduct on implicit and explicit spiritual leadership and spiritual organizational principles.

Board members, staff, customers, and government officials repeatedly commented that the culture and ambiance of CEL was highly creative, entrepreneurial, and had "something different" from other public sector organizations. When visiting the office, visitors would comment on how positive, warm, and purposeful CEL feels. CEL's stakeholders and customers had confidence in CEL. Customers' feedback marked CEL staff as respectful, deeply passionate, highly professional, and quick to admit and correct mistakes.

This chapter will provide further evidence that CEL was indeed a high performance organization. Then CEL's commitment to sustainability is dis-

Spiritual Leadership in Action, pages 103–120
Copyright © 2013 by Information Age Publishing

cussed, which, coupled with its emphasis on employee wellbeing and high performance, further established CEL as an organization dedicated to maximizing the triple bottom line through spiritual leadership. Next is an overview of balanced scorecards and the spiritual leadership balanced scorecard business model as an approach to measure and verify triple bottom line performance. Finally, we offer CEL's balanced scorecard as an example of an organization that moved toward implementing this business model.

CEL as a High Performance Organization

In addition to the research project covered in the previous chapter, additional independent studies were carried out by Oakleigh Consulting and by Mango Research that supported the assertion that CEL was a high-performing organization.

The Oakleigh Study

An independent review by Oakleigh Consulting Group (2007) found that CEL improved individual and organizational performance. They analyzed formal inspection reports of 74 FE colleges and skills providers and discovered a high correlation between CEL engagement and improved middle and senior management motivation and performance, as well as a higher capacity for continuous improvement.

The Oakleigh review concluded that CEL had succeeded in facilitating the debate about leadership, governance, and diversity issues within the FE sector by reaching more people and engaging with those who took leadership development seriously. Leadership development activities had a positive impact on student satisfaction, retention, and achievement rates in FE colleges. There was also evidence at senior management levels that the increased motivation, morale, and confidence from their CEL experience filtered through to other parts of their organizations.

As reported by participants, CEL's approaches to leadership development had helped bring about changes to personal attitudes, capabilities, and behavior. They thought and felt differently and more confidently as leaders than they did previously. Participants could identify changes in their day-to-day action and behavior that helped improve performance.

The Mango Research Study

A study conducted by Mango Research (2007) found that CEL was perceived as a leadership expert: delivering strategic approaches and tools, influencing policy, and supporting the quality agenda for the FE sector. Mango reported the following as representative of the statements made by interviewees:

CEL seizes leadership. (Stakeholder)

... to bring leadership as a core concept in the sector. (Customer)

Raising standards of leadership in FE. (Stakeholder)

CEL has established a concept of excellence and raised the sights of most FE colleges. Has put a whole emphasis on leadership. (Customer)

CEL are playing a unique role in the sector—plenty of leadership courses around but not tailored to FE needs. (Stakeholder)

CEL's impact in raising quality of management and leadership in the sector is hugely important. (Stakeholder)

Leadership and management development is fundamental to the delivery of our strategic plan. The Roots to Treetops program has more than exceeded our expectations and in particular has been delivered in a very challenging, supportive and enjoyable way. (Vicki Fagg, Principal, College of North West London)

I am delighted to be in the first cohort to undertake the principal's qualifying program. Running a college is an important and challenging role, and I fully support the introduction of a program that recognizes the professionalism of a vibrant FE sector. (Stephen Grix, Principal, Mid Kent College)

CEL's internal performance indicators were also consonant with the attributes of a good employer:

- Salary and bonuses were in many cases above the sector average.
- Development funds were considerably greater than the norm for the higher education sector, let alone the further education sector.
- Due attention was accorded to personal and professional development and to mentoring and coaching.
- There was a strong emphasis on equality of opportunities and on creating a work environment imbued with respect for the individual and their particular needs and interests.

What Made CEL a High-Performing organization?

The last major study published by CEL in May 2008, *CEL as a High Performing Organization* (2008b), concluded that there was sufficient and consistent evidence to suggest that CEL was a successful, high performing organization. This study cited the independent validation of high customer satisfaction levels, brand reputation, leader development, and organizational improvement as well as praise from senior ministers.

The consistent evidence for CEL's high performance invited the question: Why? A study conducted by the Institute for Corporate Productivity in the USA reported the findings of a survey of 1,369 American respondents about a series of organizational characteristics that literature suggested were associated with high performance. The study found that higher-performing organizations were superior to their lower performing counterparts in a number of areas. Many of these organizational characteristics were demonstrated by CEL.

- Their philosophies are consistent with their strategies, and their strategies were more consistent, clearer, and well thought out.
- They were more likely to go above and beyond for their customers. They strived to be world-class in providing customer value, thought hard about customers' future and long-term needs, and exceeded customer expectations. Customer needs were a high priority, and they were more likely to see customer information as the most important factor for developing new products and services.
- They adhered to high ethical standards throughout the organization.
- Their leaders were more likely to promote the best people for the job, make sure that performance expectations were clearly communicated, and convinced employees that their behaviors affected the success of the organization.
- They were superior in training people on the job and enabling employees to work well together.
- Their employees thought the organization was a good place to work and expressed readiness to meet new challenges and commit to innovation. Employees used their skills, knowledge, and experience to create unique solutions for customers.

Demographics and personal histories. CEL's population included experienced senior managers (in their forties) and young juniors (in their twenties). Anecdotal evidence suggested that a number of them were survivors of previous work environments where they had endured frustrating work-related experiences. It seems that the combination of youthful energy and frustrated past experiences, within a supportive environment, were part of a recipe for high performance. CEL was an intimate organization where people knew each other and interacted informally and frequently in one common open space. Therefore, the combination of size, space, and informality seemed to contribute to CEL's high performance.

Challenge: External versus internal. CEL itself was conceived in turbulence and eventually reborn, and it faced daunting challenges in its first years of operation. These included shaping an identity and brand, differentiating itself in the sector (and other markets), and becoming financially self-sufficient. These challenges were translated internally to stretch personal objectives. The matching of external challenge (threat) and internal challenge (stretch) was key to CEL's high performance.

Identification. CEL was a model for both personal and organizational spiritual leadership, with a strong emphasis on serving the sector. Identification with this mission was an essential driver of high performance.

Feedback. CEL sought constant feedback from customers on the delivery of its products and services. Feedback on individual performance was also available internally through performance assessment, personal development objectives, and informally through interaction with peers. The availability of this feedback, processed within a supportive environment, was a key to achieving organizational objectives that contributed to high performance.

Spiritual leadership and its impact on wellbeing at CEL. Observations and discussions from the interviews and focus groups suggested high employee wellbeing at CEL. This was validated in the spiritual leadership survey discussed in the previous chapter.

CEL's Focus on Sustainability and Sustainable Development

CEL placed a major emphasis on sustainability as part of its commitment to the triple bottom line. The FE colleges had already stated a public commitment to support sustainability. Lynne and CEL believed that there was a need for leaders at all levels within the learning and skills sector to sponsor, drive, endorse, and support sustainability and sustainable development as part of their commitment to the triple bottom line.

The people at CEL felt they had an important role to play in embedding sustainable development in all CEL programs as an integral element of leadership development. In its strategy for sustainable development, *Toward Leadership for Sustainability: The CEL Sustainable Development Strategy* (CEL, 2007d, p. 8), CEL defined sustainability as "a state of existence where social well-being and quality of life is maintained without degrading the ecological systems upon which life depends." Sustainable development is "development which meets the needs of the present without compromising the ability of future generations to meet their own needs." It is therefore a process whereby one assesses the social, environmental, and economic aspects of any action or decision in order to achieve an outcome that is as close to sustainability as possible.

CEL believed that leadership support and development was essential for the implementation of sustainability and sustainable development. In shaping its role and contribution to the sustainable development agenda, CEL identified a pressing need for FE leaders to support sustainable development in their organizations and teams as well as to be equipped with the knowledge, skills, and understanding to provide that leadership.

CEL also believed that there was a need for leaders at all levels within further education colleges to sponsor, drive, endorse, and support sustainability and sustainable development activity as part of their commitment to their own triple bottom line. Many staff in CEL had a huge passion for this topic. Two staff members, in particular, had expertise and phenomenal energy and commitment to drive the sustainability agenda and to involve and inspire all CEL staff to be role models for sustainability as well as encouraging sector leaders. Conrad Benefield and Trisha Roberts, as sustainability champions, were a powerful example of staff taking the initiative, with full autonomy and backing from the senior managers, to ensure that CEL itself modeled sustainability in its own office environment.

The FE colleges had already stated a public commitment to support sustainability, and many colleges were exemplars of good practice in this arena. The people at CEL believed they had an important role to play in embedding sustainable development in all CEL programs as an integral element of leadership development. In *Leadership for Sustainability: Making Sustainable Development a Reality for Leaders* (2007a, p. 10), CEL defined such leadership as "promoting and supporting sustainable development principles in all aspects of the role of the individual leader and the organization."

CEL initially met with leaders and other interested stakeholders that supported sustainability to develop an understanding of the relationships between sustainable development and leadership. CEL's sustainable development strategy emerged from two research projects, a sustainability conference, and a consultation seminar. It was presented at the House of Lords in November 2007. The strategy set out how CEL would support FE leaders in developing their capability to be "leaders for sustainability" by building CEL's capacity for sustainability, partnerships with key stakeholders that were committed to sustainable development, leadership capability for developing sustainable organizations, and sustainability practices by leading, supporting, and contributing to the ongoing debate and discussion concerning leadership for sustainability.

From the beginning, CEL sought to engage and collaborate with their strategic partners in the development of a sustainability strategy. As one of the founding members of the Sustainability Integration Group (SIGnet), CEL benefited from the insights and experiences of a range of colleagues from across further and higher education, many of whom were in the process of developing, or were implementing, sustainable development action plans. Those partners were among the first to hear and comment on CEL's earliest thinking on a sustainable development strategy. As work on the strategy progressed, valuable partnerships were established, most notably with the Learning and Skills Council.

CEL's model for sustainable development is illustrated in Figure 8.1. In supporting the embedding of sustainable development in the learning and skills sector, CEL identified four distinct but inter-related objectives that provided the foundation for CEL's activities in this area.

- Build CEL—Develop CEL's own capacity and practice both to support other organizations and to become more sustainable itself.
- Build leadership—Support the development of leaders' and organizations' capacity and capability to be leaders for sustainability.
- Build partnership—Actively contribute to policy development and practice in sustainable development at the sector level.
- Build practice—Lead, support, and contribute to debate, discussion, and improvement in leadership for sustainability.

While leadership was a core theme of CEL's strategy for sustainable development, at its heart was the development of learners' knowledge, skills, and qualities to understand and demonstrate sustainable development as citizens, often described as "sustainability literacy." Leaders at all levels in the sector played an instrumental role in making this happen. Building CEL was desirable in itself, but its main purpose for sustainable development was that it would make CEL better equipped to meet the other three objectives. By building practice, CEL would build leadership. Building partnerships would improve the quality and impact of everything that the leaders from CEL's programs do to achieve the other objectives. Leaders and partners could then work to implement sustainable development strategies that influence sector teaching and learning, learners, employers and their operations, and the communities they serve.

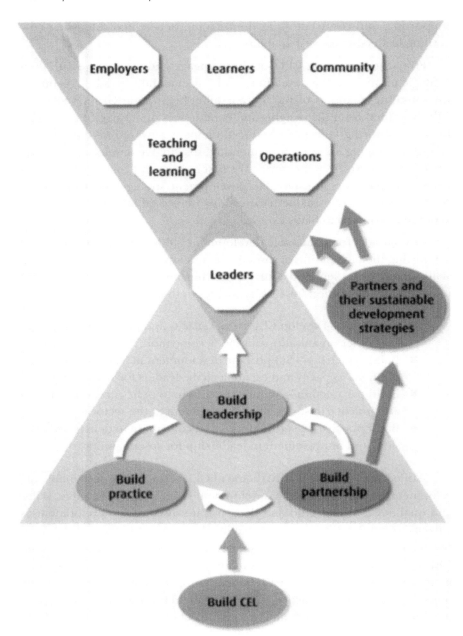

Figure 8.1 CEL's model for sustainable development.

CEL Moves toward the Spiritual Leadership Balanced Scorecard Business Model

One of the greatest challenges facing leaders in both the public and private sectors today is to generate profits and revenue growth and score high on other metrics of performance excellence while simultaneously improving the lives of employees and the communities in which they operate—the triple bottom line. These organizations are increasingly being held responsible for the impact their activities have on employees, suppliers, customers, and the communities. They must account not only to shareholders and investors but also to politicians, the media, employees, community groups, government agencies, environmentalists, and human rights organizations. This trend has fundamentally changed the operating environment for organizational leaders. A positive triple bottom line reflects an increase in the organization's value, including its human and societal capital as well as its profitability and economic growth. It can serve as a balanced scorecard that captures in numbers and words the degree to which any organization is, or is not, creating value for its shareholders, employees, customers, and other key stakeholders.

Kaplan and Norton introduced the Balanced Scorecard in 1992 in their classic Harvard Business Review article, "The balanced scorecard—Measures that drive performance." They provided a framework for capturing metrics at the executive level based on the four categories of customer satisfaction, financial performance, internal processes, and employee learning and growth. Non-financial measures provide the balance needed to supplement financial measures and align employees with strategy. Although specific measures will vary across organizations, there are generic, core outcome measures such as customer satisfaction, financial data, and employee skills that are common across strategies and industries. The non-financial measurement categories—customers, internal business processes, and learning and growth—represent an investment in intangible assets that build the capabilities for a company's future growth.

An example of a balanced scorecard is shown in Figure 8.2. A balanced scorecard's strategic areas of focus are derived from an organization's strategic management process. The actual scorecard reports strategic performance indicators in those areas of focus that have been derived from the firm's strategic plan and for which quantifiable performance objectives have been established. For example, for the learning and growth category, five core outcome measurements are identified: employee wellbeing, or-

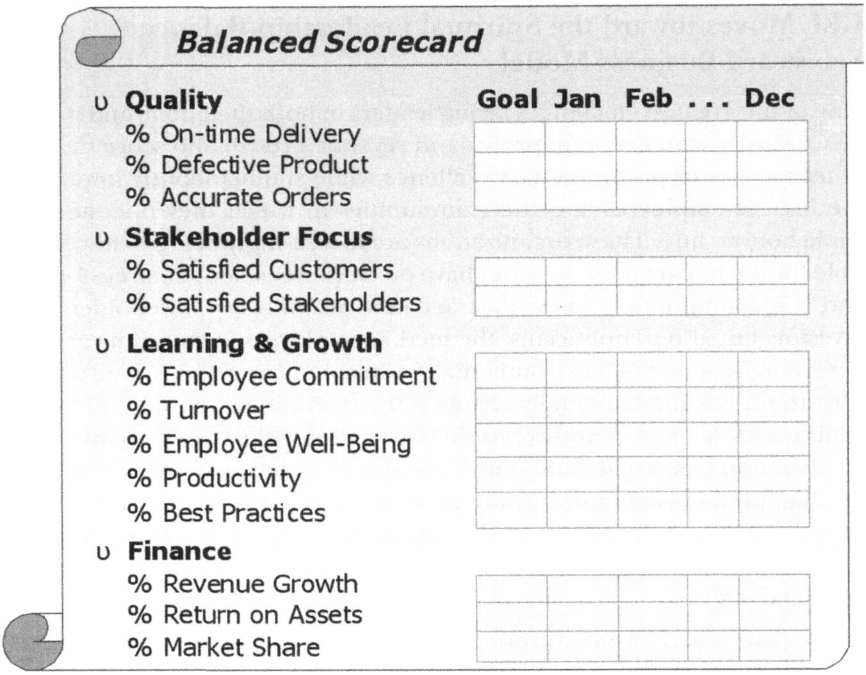

Balanced Scorecard

	Goal	Jan	Feb	...	Dec
ᴜ **Quality**					
% On-time Delivery					
% Defective Product					
% Accurate Orders					
ᴜ **Stakeholder Focus**					
% Satisfied Customers					
% Satisfied Stakeholders					
ᴜ **Learning & Growth**					
% Employee Commitment					
% Turnover					
% Employee Well-Being					
% Productivity					
% Best Practices					
ᴜ **Finance**					
% Revenue Growth					
% Return on Assets					
% Market Share					

Figure 8.2   Balanced scorecard.

ganizational commitment, retention or turnover, employee productivity, and implementation of best practices. By examining monthly trend data and performance versus targets, performance gaps can be identified that, if closed, may provide the firm with competitive advantage.

Such a balanced scorecard approach is offered by the spiritual leadership balanced scorecard business model, given in Figure 8.3, which places major emphasis on maximizing the triple bottom line through spiritual leadership (Fry & Nisiewicz, 2013). The strategic management process is initiated with the development of a vision of service to key stakeholders through a culture based on altruistic love. This, coupled with an internal and external stakeholder analysis, forms the foundation for developing strategic objectives and action plans. These then are the source for the leading and lagging indicators that comprise the organization's balanced scorecard performance categories.

Leading indicators and metrics are used to measure the performance of ongoing company operations. Generally, the more strategic the level of the scorecard in the organizational chart, the more results-oriented and

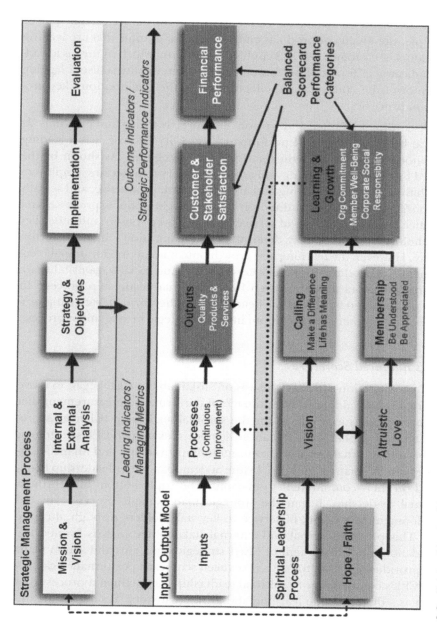

Figure 8.3 Spiritual leadership balanced scorecard business model.

lagging are the specific measures that are reported in the scorecard. In Figure 8.3, these measures comprise the quality, customer and stakeholder satisfaction, and financial balanced scorecard performance categories. For example, the quality of products and services are outputs that are leading indicators of customer and stakeholder satisfaction, which in turn is a leading indicator of financial performance. However, quality is also a lagging indicator of the efficiency and effectiveness of the organization's key production processes.

According to Kaplan and Norton, employee learning and growth is *the* central balanced scorecard performance category because it is a leading indicator that drives the other performance categories. As shown by the dotted line from the learning and growth category to processes, employees who have a sense of wellbeing and are committed, productive, and socially responsible will strive to continuously improve organizational processes and produce quality products and services that satisfy customers and other key stakeholders who, ultimately, determine the organization's financial performance. However, the learning and growth outcomes of organizational commitment and productivity, employee wellbeing, and social responsibility are lagging indicators that are driven by the spiritual leadership process. In turn, as illustrated by the double headed arrow, the spiritual leadership process is driven by and provides input into the strategic management process.

CEL's Balanced Scorecard

In conjunction with its emphasis on sustainability, CEL began to move toward a balanced scorecard approach of performance measurement that can be viewed as a prototype for the spiritual leadership balanced scorecard business model. CEL's balanced scorecard examined CEL's customer, people and internal processes, continuous improvement, and financial categories. Referencing Figure 8.3, Lynne Sedgmore and her leadership team, based on their commitment to maximize the triple bottom line through spiritual leadership, began the strategic management process with the development of a vision, of service to key stakeholders through altruistic love. This plus an internal and external stakeholder analysis formed the foundation for development of CEL's strategic objectives and action plans that provided the basis for CEL's balanced scorecard performance categories. CEL's commitment to spiritual leadership also defined a process that acted as a driver for the learning and growth category (results for organizational commitment, productivity, and life satisfaction were reported in Chapter 7). In turn CEL's spiritual leadership process informed and was influenced by CEL's strategic management process.

Performance measures were developed for all internal programs as well as for key external stakeholders as part of the development of CEL's balanced scorecard. Due to space limitations, only the major critical results for the key focus areas of customers, people and internal business processes, continuous improvement, and financial performance for the second quarter of 2008 are given in Table 8.1. CEL had a green light status for their balanced scorecard customer, internal business process, continuous improvement, and financial balanced scorecard performance categories during this period (Centre for Excellence in Leadership, 2008a).

TABLE 8.1   CEL's Balanced Scorecard

Balance Scorecard Quarter 1: April–June 2008

Key to color coding

Goals and Measures		Traffic Light Indicators	
Critical		Green	
Desirable		Amber	
		Red	

1. **The customer perspective:** CEL as a public sector organization existed to provide services that met the policy imperatives of government and the needs of stakeholders and customers. It was critical that CEL had clear strategies for meeting customer needs and, in turn, had performance measures that helped assess customer and stakeholder expectations, perceptions, and levels of satisfaction. Such measures assisted CEL in retaining a clear customer focus on such expectations by tracking performance in meeting them.

Customer Perspective

By this we mean the perspectives of the institutions and individuals that we serve. To be successful, how should we appear to our customers and key stakeholders?

Goals	Measures	Indicators
Overall Customer satisfaction is achieved	Target 85% in line with DfES requirements	98% customer satisfaction achieved
Participants recognize CEL as delivering programs, services, and interventions that meet their specific needs	% of CEL participants describing their experience as good or very good	98% customer satisfaction achieved
Customers consider CEL to be a value for money supplier	Average % of CEL customers describing the services received as "good" or "very good" value for money in relation to the services provided increasing year on year	98% customer satisfaction achieved; Reduced contractor overheads achieved

(continued)

TABLE 8.1 CEL's Balanced Scorecard (continued)

CEL is seen as actively supporting and promoting diversity	Numbers using CEL subsidy; strong diversity strategy; number of individuals from under-represented groups participating in CEL programs and services	For the first quarter 283 individual subsidies have been granted, a record high for a first quarter

2. **The people and internal business process perspective (Learning and Growth):** To provide quality and cost-effective services and value for money. CEL identified the key people and business processes it needed to be good at and then measured its performance in undertaking those processes. This perspective encouraged CEL's directors and managers to identify performance of the key business processes in the context of overall strategy, to assess current performance in undertaking those processes, and to establish targets for improving performance.

Internal Business Process Perspective
To be successful, which business processes should we be good at?

Goals	Measures	Indicators
Quality Assurance	Year on year reduction on % of non-compliances in quality audits and % of customer complaints; year on year increase in compliments	0 formal complaints
Appoint, retain, and develop high quality employees and associates	% of recruitment offers declined; annual employee/associate turnover rate; average number of training interventions per capita; internal promotions as % of all appointments; sickness rates	In this quarter we have had 4 new starters and 5 leavers = turnover rate of 7.6% 6 new roles were offered, 2 of which were internal transfers and 0 were internal promotions.
Promote diversity at all levels and roles in the organization	Workforce monitoring in relation to national benchmarks of ethnicity, gender, age and disability	Internal monitoring reveals our workforce average for this quarter is: 73.5 % Female 88% Full time 69% White British/Irish/ Any other White background

(continued)

TABLE 8.1   CEL's Balanced Scorecard (continued)

3. **The continuous improvement perspective:** To achieve continuous improvement, with a learning organization perspective, in delivering quality and cost-effective services, CEL needed to ensure that it was able to learn and to improve from both an individual and organizational perspective to demonstrate value for money. It was important to measure CEL's ability to learn, to cope with change, and to improve through its people, its systems, and its infrastructure.

Continuous Improvement Perspective

To be successful, how will we sustain our ability to learn and to improve?

Goals	Measures	Indicators
Sector ownership of CEL	Evidence gathered from stakeholders across the learning and skills sector via a wide and inclusive range of intelligence gathering activities will enable CEL to be innovative and creative in the creation and development of programs and services for 2006 to 2008	Quarterly meeting of CEL's advisory group and ongoing interactions with the sector inform development—repeat business levels increased
Achievement of value for money is proactive and on-going	Business planning and performance review is at the heart of the regular monitoring and evaluation of the objectives and activities contained in the 2006 to 2008 business plan to ensure that a process of continuous quality improvement is proactive and ongoing	Open tender process initiated March, 2007 to achieve improved quality and value for money
CEL's contribution to the development of the FE system is effectively articulated in the improvement strategy coordinated by QIA.	Activities accurately presented in the improvement strategy; CEL's status as a key partner is clear.	CEL has contributed to the improvement strategy through their relationship with QIA and is working towards the new organization, LSIS

4. **The financial perspective:** CEL required key measures of its financial performance, but again, these needed to be directly linked to overall goals and help CEL from being solely financially driven to mission driven.

Financial Perspective

To be successful, how should we appear to those who provide our financial resources?

Goals	Measures	Indicators
Deliver to CEL's annual budget agreed by the board	Difference of income over expenditure; Positive cash flow	Estimated full year is surplus of £118k against budget of £65k.

(continued)

TABLE 8.1   CEL's Balanced Scorecard (continued)

Diversify income streams	Maximize share of college market; Increase market share of developing markets in ACL and WBL to achieve financial self sufficiency incrementally year on year	CEL has or is engaged with over 300 of the 389 FE colleges, representing in excess of 75% of all FE colleges.
Work towards financial self-sufficiency	Return from sales meets a greater % of CEL's operational overhead costs	The year to date dependency on DfES Strategic Project grant was 49%, which is against the budgeted figure of 58%.
Ensure that all programs and services achieve contribution set out in annual business plan	Monthly review and quarterly reconciliation at business planning meetings.	The overall budgeted contribution target of 34.2% at the end of Q3 was exceeded with an actual total contribution of 36.8%.

Major outcomes as of April 2008, included:

- growth to 80 full-time staff and 250 part-time associates;
- customer satisfaction of 98%;
- nearly 40,000 participants through CEL in five years;
- surplus of £1m in 2006/2007, surplus of £1.5m in 2007/2008—all reinvested in the further development of CEL's activities;
- 32 product and service offerings;
- organizational spiritual leadership and stakeholder perception surveys very positive;
- overall budget at £16m annually in 2006/2007 and 2007/2008;
- financial dependency reduced to 49%;
- high staff morale;
- strong stakeholder engagement, satisfaction, and high regard;
- powerful impact studies on CEL's impact on college performance and inspection results; and
- high and positive media profile.

Conclusion

Several independent studies confirmed that CEL had recovered from the difficulties associated with the original consortium of partners and established itself as a premier provider of leadership programs for the learning and skills sector. At the heart of this success was Lynne's emphasis on personal and organizational spiritual leadership as central to employee wellbeing and performance excellence. CEL's approach to leadership development had helped bring about changes to personal attitudes, capabilities, and behaviors as reported by participants, who stated that its leadership development programs had a positive impact on student satisfaction, retention, and achievement rates in FE colleges. The Principal's Qualifying Program was a highly flexible and personalized learning program that was recognized for supporting FE principals in leading complex change.

CEL also made a strong commitment to embed the sustainability aspect of the triple bottom line as a vital element in its leadership programs. CEL worked with its partners to build sustainable development strategies and action plans that would serve the needs of FE colleges committed to support sustainable development in their organizations and teams. These consultations produced CEL's model for sustainable development, which provided a framework to guide development of its sustainable development leadership programs and initiatives.

As CEL became ever more committed to maximizing the triple bottom line, Lynne and her leadership team found the need to move toward a balanced scorecard approach for performance measurement. CEL's balanced scorecard, which was a prototype of the spiritual leadership balanced scorecard business model, assumed that the learning and growth of employees is the leading indicator that drives other performance categories. Results based on measuring their customer, people and internal business processes, continuous improvement, and financial performance categories provided further evidence that CEL was indeed a high performance organization that maximized the triple bottom line through spiritual leadership.

Practical Tools

For those interested in maximizing the triple bottom line, the major tools introduced in this chapter include:

1. *Sustainability*—Emphasizes a state of existence and (business) conduct where social wellbeing and quality of life is maintained without degrading the ecological systems upon which life depends.

2. *Sustainable development*—Focuses on development that meets the needs of the present without compromising the ability of future generations to meet their own needs.

3. *Model for sustainable development*—Specifies a process whereby organizations can assess the social, environmental, and economic aspects of any action or decision in order to achieve an outcome that is as close to sustainability as possible.

4. *Balanced scorecard categories*—Provides an overall framework or set of categories for establishing a performance measurement system to ensure that strategies are balanced and that financial results are driven by employee learning and growth, quality products and services, and customer and stakeholder satisfaction.

5. *Spiritual leadership balanced scorecard business model*—Utilizes organizational spiritual leadership as the driver of the balanced scorecard categories to maximize the triple bottom line.

9

The Legacy of CEL

A s all this success for CEL was being applauded, a threatening political scenario was unfolding: published in 2005, the Foster Report entitled *Realizing the potential: A review of the future role of further education colleges* had proposed that the whole learning and skills landscape was too complex, with far too many intermediary national organizations, and that it had to be simplified. The term "the galaxy of stars" was coined by Foster, and a search to reduce the number of national organizations became a political imperative. Senior civil servants were also given the mission to reduce the number of national quasi-autonomous, non-governmental organizations (quangos) as soon as possible, a move that eventually resulted in the elimination or merger of over 200 of them. Although not technically a quango, CEL was one of the very early targets of this approach.

The Merger of CEL

Based on the Foster Report, the roles of CEL and another national sector organization, the Quality Improvement Agency (QIA) that focused on quality improvement, were examined. A merger of CEL and QIA became a po-

Spiritual Leadership in Action, pages 121–134
Copyright © 2013 by Information Age Publishing
121

litical option within a context of simplification, desired efficiencies, a focus on shared services, and a performance review of QIA. Another reason given for the merger was that CEL had not achieved financial self-sufficiency as was originally planned. A merger not only met the mandate of the Foster Report but could, in addition to the issues related to CEL's continued government funding, also deal with the emerging issue of what to do with QIA. The politics dictated that a solution had to be found and quickly. Based on this political context it soon became clear that this merger was imperative.

CEL subsequently was ordered by the Department for Innovation, Universities, and Skills (DIUS) to enter into a complex and difficult merger with QIA, which had a much larger annual budget of £125m (CEL's was £16m per year) and a very different and highly bureaucratic culture and mindset. DIUS was a UK government department created in 2007 to take over some of the functions of the Department of Education and Skills and of the Department of Trade and Industry. In June 2009 it was merged into the newly formed Department for Business, Innovation and Skills, (BIS). At the time DIUS was responsible for adult learning, some parts of further education, higher education, as well as skills related to science and innovation. One of its strategic objectives was to strengthen the capacity, quality, and reputation of the further and higher education systems and institutions to support national economic and social needs.

Each organization began to see the other in critical and stereotypical ways; CEL viewed QIA as rigid, slow, and overly fixated on bureaucratic process to the detriment of creativity and speed, and QIA viewed CEL as a renegade and weak on systems and procedures. It became clear to Lynne and her team that the civil servants within DIUS believed that the activities of CEL were considered "too adventurous," out of sync, and counter cultural to mainstream and traditional public sector organizations under their purview.

CEL's notable achievements, its high profile, and strong stakeholder support were also seen as a threat by other organizations. In their political naivety and over self-confidence, the CEL leadership team missed the warning signs that civil servants were withdrawing support from CEL and giving leadership budgets, resources, and responsibilities to other organizations. Ultimately, CEL's superior performance claims became questioned as well as the accuracy of the data provided by CEL, despite clear evidence to the contrary. The independence and competence of some of the external assessments and assessors were also questioned. All these were signs that lack of trust was beginning to be an issue for CEL's key funders.

Lynne and her staff embraced the belief that their high performance, customer satisfaction, and stakeholder support would protect them from this political storm. Their advisory group also missed that the politics to reduce the number of national organizations would negatively affect CEL. The CEL board and advisory group were adamant and vocal in also defending CEL, but it some became clear that, despite all this support and effort, the merger was inevitable.

After much discussion and pressure, both QIA and CEL agreed to merge. To bring about a successful merger DIUS commissioned two sets of consultants to oversee the merger and guide the process of its implementation. Their confidential reports highlighted the extreme differences in cultures of QIA and CEL and saw this as the main challenge and area of conflict. To work through this a 12 month program of joint meetings was initiated to explore and overcome differences and, as part of this effort, co-create a mutual vision for the new organization.

One of the ways in which CEL's senior team and staff coped with the stress of the situation was to focus on the most exciting part of the merger: the emergence of a new form of organization. What CEL did not want was yet another example of superficial structural change. Lynne and her team decided to give the new merged organization their full support. The CEL board and senior team avoided the temptation to resist the merger and decided to embrace a new organizational model while ceding control and committing to working with the QIA management to create a new self-regulated, responsive, powerful, and successful organization to serve the larger good of the sector.

It was on this basis that CEL, with the confidence of five successful years, consented to shelve its desire to maintain CEL as a separate entity and agreed to support the formation of a radical new merged organization. For anything less the pain and loss would have been too great. CEL's vision became to co-create a new organization with a customer-centered focus and linked to the wisdom and expertise of sector professionals. It would be geared to what was happening on the front line and to the genuine needs of sector leaders and professionals.

As part of this effort, they fought for what they held most dear in the CEL culture and values. To assist in this effort CEL brought in Don Beck, the founder of Spiral Dynamics, to assist Lynne and the CEL senior team with their work on merging the values, culture, and initial stage of development of the two organizations. He helped them understand the key cultural differences, why CEL leaders and staff were experiencing such a threat to CEL's continued existence, and their own shortcomings as well as successes.

The board was very supportive at difficult moments; for example, supporting office relocation, planned before the merger, despite reluctance from DIUS

In spite of this commitment to positive cultural change, it turned out the two organizations' cultures were so very different that they could not dialogue or work together effectively. In the end consultants, staff meetings, constant dialogues, and new CEOs were unable to resolve the fundamental differences in vision, values, culture, and business practices between the two organizations. The QIA agency's primary focus was on quality improvement programs for practitioners. It was highly bureaucratic with formalized procurement procedures and slow to respond to innovative requests, although they were recognized for offering helpful interventions to individual organizations and received good customer feedback. CEL was primarily customer-focused and more adaptable and responsive to individual needs with processes and formal procedures that CEL viewed as adequate to the task, and no more. The CEL senior team philosophy was to only introduce procedures as were necessary to make the business effective, not the other way round. Although audit reports were good with high customer satisfaction and performance ratings, from the more powerful QIA bureaucratic perspective these were viewed as less important.

The criticism that CEL failed to comply sufficiently with detailed and bureaucratic procedures and processes was one that proved fatal for CEL as the merger progressed. While CEL's exceptional accomplishments and profitability were acknowledged by stakeholders, learners, and the Ministers, the DIUS (who also had a core civil service bureaucratic mentality) began to view CEL negatively due to failure to adhere to bureaucratic processes and a perceived lack of commitment to the merger. For example, a major issue of disagreement became the lease on a new building. Despite the merger (which was expected to unfold over two years), the existent CEL offices had become too small and were of low quality. In order to lift the spirits of staff and to ensure continued high performance, the CEL board and senior team felt it vital that new offices with adequate facilities were of paramount importance.

On October 1, 2008, CEL and the QIA merged to form a new organization dedicated to supporting excellence and leadership development in the further education and skills sector. CEL became part of the Learning and Skills Improvement Service (LSIS) with a new chair, board, and CEO. Five of the original CEL senior team stayed on as members of the LSIS senior team. CEL's chair, Lynne (CEO), the deputy CEO, and finance director all decided not to go forward into the new organization thereby facilitating a brand new beginning with new blood.

A new CEO of the forthcoming LSIS was appointed in February 2008 but after an initial assessment of the role decided not to take up the appointment. An interim CEO was assigned to the role for three months, from March to June. A third CEO was then appointed in June 2008 following a national search. The third CEO left in August 2009, and a fourth interim CEO was put in place without a national search. A new, fifth CEO was appointed in March, 2011 following a national recruiting effort and is still in place at the time of writing, although LSIS funding will cease in August 2013, necessitating its closure.

Mergers are very time consuming. However, CEL managed to continue exceeding its performance goals and produced an even bigger surplus than planned. CEL's culture seemed to strengthen during this period; the away days became even more outstanding, and sessions of appreciation and celebration were numerous. Leading up to the merger, several parties, picnics, and farewell CEL events were organized to mark the passing of the organization. These were always a mix of joy at being together, the pain of inevitable death, and the need to move on.

A particularly poignant statement on the move from CEL to LSIS was put thus by a negatively affected member of staff:

> In CEL I felt I was in a sunny garden, growing, flowering and in a creative, beautiful garden. Now I am in a dark, dank potting shed—a very painful place.

Others were able to adapt more easily and to see advantages:

> While it was good in CEL, you have to move on; there are good things in LSIS and lots of good people doing their best; my energies are now focused on making LSIS work.

The last act of CEL was highly symbolic. All staff received a Silver Star paper weight as a gift to mark the end of the CEL era with a note saying "thanks for being a CEL star and best wishes for the future." CEL also bought a star in the sky and named it the "CEL star" with everyone receiving a certificate of exactly where this star is in the stellar constellation so that people can orientate themselves to it and be reminded of CEL at any time, wherever they may be. Many of the respondents of the post-mortem questionnaire referred to it in reply to the question: If you were to leave an artifact or a vignette of CEL in a time capsule for future generations, what would that be?

The Legacy of CEL

The leadership team, staff, and board of CEL were very keen to articulate and leave a legacy to the merged organization in the hope of leaving the best aspects of CEL culture, performance, and approaches for other existing and future organizations. This legacy was focused through the written word and through the lived experience and spirit of CEL continuing through the people who had created and lived the reality and power of CEL's commitment to the models of organizational spirituality and spiritual leadership.

Before leaving CEL, the leadership team articulated the notion of the starfish, having read collectively the book *The Starfish and the Spider* (Brafman & Beckstrom, 2006). This is the notion that the parts of a starfish may break off, but the starfish will heal again, leaving the piece that has broken away to become a living part elsewhere but still being an inter-connected part of the original starfish. The legacy of CEL also continues in different ways through those who left CEL, including Lynne, the deputy CEO, and key members of the executive leadership team and other staff, who are still heavily committed to and passionate about CEL and the sector. The leaders and staff who have stayed and moved into the merged organization continue to support and integrate the best of CEL and their own individual professional and contribution into the new organization, LSIS.

Some agreed that they would meet regularly with the remaining ex-CEL leaders in the merged organization, which has happened. They committed also to taking the CEL energy, spirit, values, and expertise into new roles they would take up and to support each other in doing so. Their infectious passion and entrepreneurial and organizational spiritual leadership are enabling them to share their experience with others and to develop a legacy of the successes of CEL in building on the good that others have done and are doing for themselves. The key sentiment was that their experience and learning within CEL could never be taken away no matter what happened to them in the future. Many said that they had found a new way of being, a better way of behaving, and a new sense of community and energy and that they wanted to be able to manifest this for themselves and others in new places.

The merger between CEL and QIA was a challenging time to say the least and in many ways felt like another dark night of the soul for Lynne as she struggled with leaving the staff and the powerful community they had formed together. After 30 years in the FE and skills sector, Lynne started making plans to retire and move to the country. Then the offer of a job as CEO of the 157 Group came along and totally revitalized her. The 157

Group is a membership organization that represents 28 large, urban, successful, and regionally influential further education colleges in England. Committed to excellence, innovation, and achieving maximum success for the sector, the 157 Group principals are key strategic leaders in their locality who take seriously the roles of influencing policy development and implementation and improving the quality, profile, and reputation of further education.

Final Reflections of the Authors

This is not a usual book, and it does not report a case-study of a usual company. So, it is entirely in the spirit of the book that we end with final reflections. The idea is to impress on the reader that there is more to the CEL story than the evidence provided in this account may suggest. The benefits of time and hindsight have allowed some impressions to mellow, whereas others have sharpened their relief. We would like to devote our final reflections of CEL to aspects that are implicitly (though necessarily fragmentally) informed by the evidence outlined in this book.

Part of the "unusuality" of the CEL case was carrying out research there and the manner in which it took place. The commission to conduct the project came out of a meeting with Dr. Altman on another subject altogether. He was engaged in a pleasant conversation with Lynne Sedgmore when she shared her thoughts on wanting to study her organization rigorously and objectively. He agreed, rather surprised, and there and then they discussed the general parameters of a possible study and the potential price tag. She asked that he send in a detailed proposal for the formalities and internal processes involved. Only on exiting her offices and in discussions with the team he would put together for the project did it dawn on him that perhaps he didn't quite get it right. There was no "hard sell." She trusted his credentials, and there was no request to qualify methods and no demand for control of information. So he was advised by his team to go back and check that his understandings were correct, which he did. He recalls Lynne being somewhat taken aback on this reversal of client/provider exchange and his asking her questions on issues already agreed on. This led to an embarrassed apology. Of course she had ensured that their formal proposal went through due internal process for agreement and funding, but the nature of their exchange was quite different in tone, trust, and style than he was used to. It was only later that he realized that this episode was entirely in line with Lynne's remarkable openness and genuine trust, which many others, like him, found such an empowering and liberating experience.

Throughout our two-phased research and intervention project, which stretched over two years, including the time in London Dr. Fry spent with CEL as well as afterward, we were given full and unconditional access to people and documentation, were encouraged to attend meetings, and were made to feel welcome and wanted. We both recall the pleasure of being involved in this undertaking on a personal level—the privilege, as researchers who have been around organizations for a life time, to evidence the machinery and running of an "excellent" organization and the intellectual excitement of seeing spirituality at work in a non-faith-based public service organization.

In other words, our experience of CEL was unique. As such, generalizations from it are necessarily restricted. But the potential for insights about how successful spiritually oriented organizations work is much greater. It is to these insights that we turn now.

Was CEL Doomed to Failure?

As we performed our "post-mortem" examination, we came to believe that this is a cardinal question for this case study and beyond. Respondents, with the benefit of hindsight, insisted on how outstanding CEL was in so many respects. And a few who were in the know commented that the people in the Ministry, the high ranking civil servants, didn't quite "get it" in terms of how CEL was able to become so successful and maintain its success, especially on such small levels of funding.

The question that begs to be answered is this: Why was CEL not allowed to continue and prosper? And why didn't the much-venerated elite British civil service "get it"? Exploring this question may suggest some structural vulnerabilities of organizations like CEL, if we accept that CEL was indeed outstanding as well as "spiritual." It also tells us something about the climate in which public sector organizations operated in Britain in the mid 2000s.

We were not privy to the behind-the-scenes deliberations on the CEL merger decision nor to its post-factum rationale, though the idea to merge CEL with QIA was patently bizarre. This is not only because mergers are notoriously difficult to make a success of, but also because QIA was about ten times the size of CEL and by common knowledge a very different kettle of fish—bureaucratic, formalistic, slow moving, uninspiring—a very different culture from CEL's. It was established in the post-mortem examination we conducted that the new creature forged of this merger—LSIS—has practically obliterated any traces of CEL.

So that is the foreground to the question we pose. Now, let us start by qualifying the said assumptions. The evidence we presented about CEL's success, as seen by all relevant stakeholders and as withstood to external examination, is clear. True, the finance provided by the government, which towards the end if its life represented about half of all its income, meant that CEL was not independent and that the money it received had to be qualified, as all public funding does. Nevertheless, the case of "value for money" CEL provided was convincing. We also showed that there was sufficient evidence to suggest that CEL was a spiritual organization. Spiritual expressions of individuals were certainly tolerated and even encouraged, the organization's mission was referenced in spirituality-relevant terms and its *modus operandi* was sensitive to spiritual implications, spirituality-related development was provided, and CEL won an International Spirit at Work Award in recognition of all of these. However, spirituality was not imprinted on its flag, nor was it evident in the public parlance of the organization, and it certainly was not in any way enforced.

Now, why merge CEL with QIA? A clue is to be found in the response from one of our *aftermath* subjects, a senior manager with CEL with a thorough inside knowledge of the sector: "There has been a mix of desire and jealousy (which is a rather lethal combination)," she commented. That reminded us of Aesop's famous fable *Killing The Goose That Laid the Golden Eggs*, the CEL variant being that if one can obtain a small egg (CEL), how wonderful would it be to obtain a much bigger egg (CEL and QIA), and in the process, inevitably, the *secret* of the goose will have to be revealed. Possibly a logical idea except it didn't quite work out.

Second, what could mitigate a perception of CEL's success, implying its failure? To answer this question we are in search of structural features, that is, built-in vulnerabilities (internal or external) that would account against a continuous success and for ultimate failure. Two positions or claims stand out: the belief (assertion) that the CEL success "is too good to be true" (external validation) and its internal correlate that CEL righteousness as a spiritual organization "is not what it seems to be."

CEL Aftermath

CEL's demise presented an unusual opportunity in business research case-studies: an actual ending. Most reports on companies are of ongoing concerns, based on official information, often portraying the better public face of an organization. The advantage this accords us in the CEL case is the opportunity to discuss with relevant stakeholders their views and insight post-mortem, often disclosing information that either was not available at the time or not disclosable for reasons of business or personal confidentiality but with the ending of CEL is now in the public domain.

The main sources of information for our aftermath analysis are the stakeholders of CEL. We approached one third of full-time staff and a selected number of associates as well as one board member 12 months after CEL was officially dismantled. We thought that a year is an appropriate time gap for this investigation, as it is sufficiently far away to allow for a considered opinion to be formed, while it is not too long for key aspects to be forgotten. The following questions were asked:

> What have you learned and/or internalized from your time at CEL that you value:
>
> (i) On a personal level?
> (ii) About working, work behavior, team work?

We asked people to treat these questions as reflection points rather than treat them verbatim. Thirteen responses were obtained, representing a cross-section of CEL: directors, middle management, rank and file staff, associates, and one board member—necessarily this was a self-selective sample. Responses were sent confidentially to Dr. Altman, and he conducted three telephone interviews as well.

The overall reaction reflected in the responses was overwhelmingly positive. Many indicated the unique and powerful experience CEL accorded them: significant and important learning experiences about themselves, about team work, about leadership. Here are indicative excerpts:

(i) On a Personal Level

> I find that I continually think back to what I learnt and how I can take this forward in working with others ... How much more enjoyment you get from work when the atmosphere is fun and supportive and not cliquey ... During my time at CEL my confidence grew, and I grew as a person ... I learnt that people need space to grow and with the right kind of support everyone can ... If I was to choose one [learning] it is the value of giving your colleagues positive feedback and telling them when they've done a good job ... I re-learnt the value of reflective practice as a powerful tool to stimulate learning ... I was given the latitude and trust to play my role, giving guidance and being open to new ideas.

(ii) About Working, Work Behavior, Team Work, Leadership

There was something magical about CEL at its best—a leadership and culture that was created, lived and directed from "the inside out." A values-led and alchemic leadership which had a transformative effect—unlocking the contribution of staff, attracting talented creative people, enrolling others in the wider task, thinking and practice.... My greatest learning was in how people work together, respect each other, how great leadership exists and how an organization can make a difference...the openness and trust and honesty when things got tough—I believe [our] team was unique and working together we made amazing things happen...What we put in we got out, and that meant the world to everyone. This made it an exciting and passionate (albeit stressful at times) working environment.

Some suggested (assumed to be) lasting impressions that guide them in their present and future working lives, for example:

Almost every week something happens in my life either at work or at home that makes me think of my time at CEL, whether it is a situation that occurs or someone I meet, but it takes me back to thinking about CEL and how things would have been dealt with there, or what would an individual have thought of this at CEL.

Maximizing the Triple Bottom Line Through Spiritual Leadership: Making the Impossible Possible

Among the millions of organizations, once in a great while we find an organization whose performance so greatly exceeds expectations that it is difficult to believe that its level of success is what it seems. When stakeholders that define standards of what excellence represents encounter performance that markedly exceeds those standards, we are left to wonder how such an aberration is possible.

This book tells the story of an organization that reached a level of performance that was seemingly impossible given its beginnings and the task environment in which it operated. Adjectives such as "stunning, "spectacular," remarkable," "incredible," and "astonishing" may be apt descriptors. Yet it is also an account that describes how a single organization experienced a devastating loss and apparent extinction when its performance on any measure was at its peak.

This book also explains how this success occurred. It offers the key models, methods, and tools that chart how this extraordinary performance was realized. Our aim has been to help leaders interested in maximizing the triple bottom line recognize the importance of spiritual leadership in action in producing transformational change and how they can create outstanding success.

It must be pointed out that these models can be effectively utilized by a wide variety of leaders in any industry and circumstance. We hope that you will find them helpful in situations where transformational change is required, major trials are encountered, or the opportunity to do something great is present.

This story of how the impossible became possible is told from the standpoint of the people who were involved in the change. Although Lynne Sedgmore has been a major focus and her story is extraordinary, it is also a story that can serve as an exemplar for any leader willing to embrace the spiritual journey regardless of age or station in life. And the shift of consciousness that must occur to take this journey is often less dramatic than in Lynne's case. Instead it is more often what William James, in *The Varieties of Religious Experience,* calls the "educational variety" because this awareness for the need to look inward and become conscious develops slowly over a period of time.

Our story also highlights the fact that no significant successful organizational change is due to a lone heroic top leader who developed a vision on his or her own. No, this story is one whereby everyone in the organization can—in fact is expected—to lead when the situations and circumstances call for it. This call to spiritual leadership includes many interwoven activities, many stakeholders, and many heroic, and non-heroic endeavors that all combined to produce a remarkable story of success.

At the risk of gross oversimplification, we offer the key reasons for success with the following summary statement that underlines what we learned from our in-depth case study. Although the overarching leadership lessons learned from CEL may be summarized in a single statement, it does not do justice to the complexity that underlies it:

> The impossible was made possible in CEL by adopting a spiritual leadership approach to change rather than the more traditional bureaucratic approach.

CEL's success can be explained through the lens of the models of organizational spirituality (Figure 1.1), the personal and organizational spiritual leadership models (Figures 2.1 and 3.1), and the methods and tools used to implement them; it was an extraordinary success that flew in the face of the conventional wisdom of what can be done when faced with imminent collapse and working against seemingly impossible odds.

As we reported, the current projects at LSIS (the organization created through the merger of CEL and QIA) were not pursued in the same way as CEL. In fact there appears to be a regression toward the old way of bureaucratic management instead of the CEL approach based on spiritual leadership. The organizational culture of the much larger QIA organization, in particular, and the DIUS were the key resistance factors. There was a lack of innovative thinking to get the system to move to new forms of learning and to devise new ways of tackling the issues. The core essence of the success of CEL was never clarified or understood and therefore has gradually been lost, and the individuals who worked so hard to keep the CEL values and ways of working going have gradually been absorbed into the LSIS ethos and values or have left the organization.

Although our account of CEL has centered on what worked, what enabled success, and what accounted for spectacular success, we have not ignored or omitted negative or problematic factors but have reported what individuals and stakeholders associated with CEL actually stated were the focus of their activities. However, our emphasis on the success at CEL and attributing the successful outcomes to the models of organizational spirituality and spiritual leadership, and the spiritual leadership balanced scorecard business model may give rise to legitimate concerns that we have ignored contrary data or unfairly biased our case analysis toward the positive. Any story that sounds too good to be true raises questions about whether alternative explanations can account for or temper the claimed success or call into question whether success has really been achieved at all.

In this regard at least two questions should be considered. First, "what level of consensus exists that success has been achieved?" Another way to ask this question is: "success according to whom?" Second, given what constitutes success in any circumstance is context-dependent, "what were the standards on which success was judged?" In other words, the key question is: "success compared to what?"

We want to be clear that, as would be expected, there are stakeholders who considered CEL's accomplishments to be less than spectacular. After all it failed to achieve self-sufficiency and seemed to fail at following the required bureaucratic procedures so dear to its most powerful stakeholders at the end—QIA and DIUS. Plus, the fact that CEL exhibited a not-so-spiritual attitude of being prideful and vociferous about its success, and that trumpeting that workplace spirituality and spiritual leadership were key to it, was probably a significant factor in CEL's demise. On the other hand, a number of other relevant stakeholders were also in agreement and attested to CEL's level of success. The results achieved at CEL are measurable and therefore also verifiable. The qualitative and quantitative research conducted by the authors supports the proposition that CEL was a strong exemplar of spiritual leadership in action as well as an organization that maximized the triple bottom line.

Probably the main lesson to be learned here is that organizations and their leaders who wish to maximize the triple bottom line by implementing the models of organizational spirituality and spiritual leadership must be careful to understand the expectations of its key stakeholders and do what it can to meet these expectations. Above all it is important in these circumstances to practice humility and give due respect to others. This does not guarantee success, but it lessens the probability of failure.

Finally, we would argue that CEL was not a failure, regardless of what happened. The potential and relevance of workplace spirituality and spiritual leadership for maximizing the triple bottom line is not diminished. No, the analogy of the starfish recounted earlier as part of CEL's legacy applies. This is the notion that the parts of a starfish may break off, but, regardless of whether the starfish lives or dies, the piece that has broken away will live and still be a part of and have the essence of the original starfish. It is in the same vein that the people of CEL who embraced CEL's ethos are alive and well and still working to re-create, within their spheres of influence, CEL's spirit and the successes, both personal and organizational, that came with it.

References

Abrudene, P. (2007). *Megatrends 2010: The Rise of Conscious Capitalism*. Charlottesville, VA: Hampton Roads Publishing Co.

Altman, Y., Ozbilgin, M., & Wilson, E. (2007). *A study on organizational effectiveness and well being at work: CEL as a case-study*. Barcelona: ESADE, Institute of Labor Studies.

Brafman, O., & Beckstrom, R. (2006). *Starfish and the spider: The unstoppable power of leaderless organizations*. Toronto, Canada: Penguin Group.

Ashmos, D., & Duchon, D. (2000). Spirituality at work: A conceptualization and measure. *Journal of Management Inquiry, 9*(2), 134–145.

Benefiel, M. (2005). The second half of the journey: Spiritual leadership for organizational transformation. *The Leadership Quarterly, 16*(5), 723–747.

Benefiel, M. (2008). *The soul of a leader: Finding your path to success and fulfillment*. New York, NY: Crossroads Publishing.

Guilford College stakeholder engagement. (2001). Best practice case studies. *Ethical Performance,* Autumn. Retrieved January 2, 2013 from http://www.ethicalperformance.com/bestpractice/casestudy/11

CEL receives International Spirit at Work Award. (2007, December). *Centre for Excellence in Leadership Newsletter*.

Centre for Excellence in Leadership. (2005). *Faith communities toolkit*. London: Author.

Centre for Excellence in Leadership. (2006). *Dignity at work policy* (in Human Resources Manual). London: Author.

Centre for Excellence in Leadership. (2007a). *Leadership for sustainability: Making sustainable development a reality for leaders*. London: Author.

Centre for Excellence in Leadership. (2007b). *Quality assurance framework*. London: Author.

Spiritual Leadership in Action, pages 135–138

Centre for Excellence in Leadership. (2007c). *Review of CEL's impact in the FE sector*. London: Author.

Centre for Excellence in Leadership. (2007d). *Towards leadership for sustainability: The CEL development strategy*. London: Author.

Centre for Excellence in Leadership. (2008a). *Balanced scorecard: Q4 and full year review for 2007–2008*. London: Author.

Centre for Excellence in Leadership. (2008b). *CEL as a high-performing organization*. London: Author.

Foster Review for the Department for Education and Skills. (2005). *Realizing the potential: A review of the future role of further education colleges*. Retrieved from http://www.theresearchcentre.co.uk/files/docs/publications/he0039.pdf

Fry, L. (2008). Spiritual leadership: State-of-the-art and future directions for theory, research and practice. In L. Bibeman & L. Tishman, *Spirituality in business: Theory, practice and future directions* (pp. 106–124). New York, NY: Palgrave.

Fry, L., Hanna, S., Noel, M., & Walumba, F. (2011). Impact of spiritual leadership on unit performance. *The Leadership Quarterly, 22*, 259–270.

Fry, L., & Nisiewicz, M. (2013). *Maximizing the triple bottom line through spiritual leadership*. Stanford, CA: Stanford University Press.

Fry, L., Matherly, L., & Ouimet, R. (2010). The spiritual leadership balanced scorecard business model: The case of the Cordon-Bleu-Tomasso Corporation. *Journal of Management, Spirituality and Religion, 7*(4), 283–315.

Fry, L., Vitucci, S., & Cedilo, M. (2005). Transforming the Army through spiritual leadership. *The Leadership Quarterly 16*, 835–862.

The Further Education Funding Council. (2000, May). Report from the inspectorate 1999–2000: Guildford College of further and higher education. Coventry: Author. Retrieved from http://dera.ioe.ac.uk/3052/2/guildford_fhe_cyc2.pdf

Giacalone, R. A., & Jurkiewicz, C. (2003). Toward a science of workplace spirituality. In R. A. Giacalone & C. L. Jurkiewicz, *Handbook of workplace spirituality and organizational performance* (pp. 3–28). New York, NY: M. E. Sharp.

James, W. (1985). *The varieties of religious experience*. London: Penguin Classics.

Joseph, M. (2002). *Leaders and spirituality—A case study*. Unpublished doctoral dissertation, University of Surrey.

Kaplan, R., & Norton, D. (1992). The balanced scorecard—Measures that drive performance. *Harvard Business Review, 70*, 71–79.

Keating, T. (1999). *The human condition: Contemplation and transformation*. New York, NY: Paulist Press.

Mango Research. (2007). Centre for excellence in leadership customer and stakeholder perception research (Executive Summary). London: Centre for Excellence in Leadership.

Oakleigh Consulting Group. (2007). Review of CEL's impact in the FE sector. London: Centre for Excellence in Leadership.

Pfeffer, J. (2003). Business and the spirit. In R. A. Giacalone & C. L. Jurkiewicz, *Handbook of workplace spirituality and organizational performance* (pp. 29–45). New York, NY: M. E. Sharp.

Tolle, E. (2004). *The power of now: A guide to spiritual enlightenment.* Novato, CA: New World Library.

Too good for Max Clifford. (2001, November). *TES: Times Educational Supplement.* Retrieved from http://www.tes.co.uk/article.aspx?storycode=356368

Way forward for three-year planning. (2003, June). *Success for ALL.* Retrieved from http://dera.ioe.ac.uk/13557/5/success-for-all-newsletter-june-2003.pdf

Western, S., & Sedgmore, L. (2008). A privileged converstaion. *Journal of Management, Spirituality and Religion, 5*(3), 321–346.

Selected Readings

Centre for Excellence in Leadership. (2004). *Leading the way.* London: Author.

Centre for Excellence in Leadership. (2006). *An ever renewing story.* London: Author.

Centre for Excellence in Leadership. (2006). *Annual Review 2005–2006.* London: Author.

Centre for Excellence in Leadership. (2007). *Annual Review 2006–2007.* London: Author.

Centre for Excellence in Leadership. (2007). *Ordinary heroes, extraordinary company: Application for the Spirit at Work Award.* London: Author.

Centre for Excellence in Leadership. (2008). *Living spirituality in the workplace: The CEL way.* London: Author.

Fry, L. (2003). Toward a theory of spiritual leadership. *The Leadership Quarterly, 14,* 693–727.

Fry, L. (2005). Introduction to the special issue: Toward a paradigm of spiritual leadership. *The Leadership Quarterly, 16*(5), 619–622.

Fry, L. (2005). Toward a theory of ethical and spiritual well-being and corporate social responsibility through spiritual leadership. In R. Giacalone, C. Jurkiewicz, & C. Dunn, *Positive psychology in business ethics and corporate responsibility* (pp. 47–83). Greenwich, CT: Information Age Publishing.

Fry, L., & Cohen, M. (2009). Spiritual leadership as a paradigm for organizational transformation and recovery from extended work hours cultures. *Journal of Business Ethics, 84,* 265–278.

Fry, L., & Kriger, M. (2009). Towards a theory of being-centered leadership: Multiple levels of being as context for effective leadership. *Human Relations, 62*(11), 1667–1734.

Fry, L., Sedgmore, L., & Atman, Y. (2009). *Maximizing the triple bottom line through a spiritual leadership balanced scorecard business model: The CEL story.* Chicago: Academy of Management Conference.

Kaplan, R., & Norton, D. (1996). *The balanced scorecard: Translating strategy into action.* Boston, MA: Harvard Business School Press.

Kaplan, R., & Norton, D. (1996). Using the balanced scorecard as a strategic management system. *Harvard Business Review, January/February,* 75–76.

Kaplan, R., & Norton, D. (2004). *Strategy maps: Converting intangible assets into tangible outcomes.* Boston, MA: Harvard Business School Press.

Kaplan, R., & Norton, D. (2006). Transforming the balanced scorecard from performance measurement to strategic management. *Accounting Horizons, 15,* 87–104.

About the Authors

Louis (Jody) W. Fry, PhD is currently professor of management at Texas A&M University–Central Texas. In addition to spending 11 years in public and private enterprise, he has been a professor at Texas A&M University, College Station and The University of Washington. Jody is also a member of the editorial review board of *The Leadership Quarterly*, former editor of *The Journal of Management, Spirituality and Religion*, a book series editor for *Advances in Workplace Spirituality: Theory, Research, and Application*, published by Information Age Publishing, and the founder of the International Institute for Spiritual Leadership (http://www.iispiritualleadership.com). He has presented papers at national and international conferences and published in top scholarly journals including *The Leadership Quarterly, The Journal of Applied Psychology, The Journal of Business Ethics, Organizational Dynamics, The Academy of Management Journal*, and *The Academy of Management Review*. Jody has worked extensively with for-profit and non-profit organizations and is co-author of *Maximizing the Triple Bottom Line Through Spiritual Leadership*, published by Stanford University Press. His present research, consulting, and executive development interests are focused on organizational development and transformation through spiritual leadership.

Yochanan Altman, PhD is recognized for his work in international human resource management, micro organizational behavior and comparative management, in addition to his pioneering work on organizational spiritu-

Spiritual Leadership in Action, pages 139–140

ality. A chartered psychologist, Yochanan holds a doctorate in organizational anthropology. He has authored eight books and over a hundred articles published in learned journals and research books. Yochanan edited the *Journal of Managerial Psychology* (Emerald); is Founding Editor of the *Journal of Management, Spirituality and Religion* (Routledge); and European Editor of *People & Strategy* (SHRM). He is co-chair of the International Association of Management, Spirituality & Religion. During the research on this project Yochanan was visiting research professor with the Future of Work Institute at ESADE, Barcelona.

Lightning Source UK Ltd.
Milton Keynes UK
UKOW07f1804200115

244802UK00001B/2/P